poetix & prose

poems + short stories

MICHAEL MOORE

Copyright © 2024 by Michael Moore

All rights reserved.

ISBN: 978-1-7390552-1-9

No part of this publication may be reproduced, distributed, or transmitted in any form or by any means, including photocopying, recording, or other electronic or mechanical methods, without the prior written permission of the author, except as permitted by U.S. copyright law. For permission requests, contact micheal@michaelxmoore.com

The story, all names, characters, and incidents portrayed in this production are fictitious. No identification with actual persons (living or deceased), places, buildings, and products is intended or should be inferred.

First edition 2024

TABLE OF CONTENTS

POEMS 2
CAT 3
Three Chairs 4
green feathered frog 7
r o l l e r c o a s t e r 10
This Not that 12
YOUR LOVE IS SUCH A THIEF 14
Think *not* so much 16
whisperings 20
timeXdistance 25
i s o l a t i o n 29
FAR PAINTED FADED HILLS 33
In the dark 34
Bleaker Street 40
rectitude 42
night•stockings 46
b e d s k l r t s 48
s i l e n z i o 52
ALONE 54
PROSE 57
Celestial 58
Domeni 61
Bereshith 66
Where Do You Put It? 69
My Spooky Friends 73

under Observation 76
BUBBLES. 80
MOLLY MABES 86
A Kiss May Be 94
eight items or less.. 97
Flight Delayed.. 99
ABOUT DONE 109
Mulberry Bushes and Christmastime..................................... 118
Hello There 123
All The Best Laid Plans 127
Light in the Dark 130
Faintly Sundown 134
A Knock At The Door.. 136
Yon Duck 144
Desmond Dak.. 151
an emiLlyburKke 158
Acceptance.. 161
Perfect. are we? 163
About the Author 165

Many thanks for the support and encouragement from

Duncan, Tim, Angelique, Anni

and

Carroll

POEMS

CAT

cat

flat

against the counter

that

supports the sinks

cat drinks

laps

at the taps

then leaps

to the floor

through the door

tail

like a sail

set

for yet

another adventure

Three Chairs

Set here along the rim
But under the eave
Sheltered by deep
Shadows of trees

In shadowy light
We watch, I/we feel
The loss, the pain
In a fog quite unreal

The memories rich
Mostly being mine
As the three of us watch
And remember the times

That we shared
And we lived through
Such sweet memories
Remembering you

As the snow sits soft
Framing the trees
Sifting and falling
All about - but who sees?

No beauty here, now
It's lost, 'cause she's gone
Our tears and their tracks
And the memories live on

Silent soft weeping
Each to one another
Hands seeking hands
Seeking each other

The light of this day
Slowly finding its end
For me, you my lover
For them, their true friend

The light of this day
Slowly finding its end
For me, you my lover
For them, their true friend

As we sit, humbly here
In a mist of deep caring
Collectively grieving
Blindly staring

In a sense of abandon
Being a place of no place
Aching searches for links
And attempts to replace

Spirit – that spirit,
So uniquely your own
Enshrouding us now
With this blanket unknown

How could this happen
To you, in whose grace
We laughed, we lingered
Here, in this place

Set here on the rim
But under the eave
Un-sheltered here, grasping
Trying to retrieve

A connection again,
Painfully to you

A bond to your soul
To help get us through

Three Adirondack chairs
Where there used to be four
Three chairs, now, only
Forever more.

green feathered frog

the green feathered frog
spoke to the blue spangled bird
'seriously, really - I've heard
not a word

'as things appear now
'tis just quite absurd"

the crickets were cranking
their cacophonous song
a silence sat heavy
'till the fox came along

'what are we here now
all talking about?
the frog spoke up
'we're trying to figure out"

'why such a mystery?
Why such confusion?
possibly might
there be some collusion?

'tween those who have standing
which most of us don't
and them that have reasons
or them who just won't

step to the front
to strike a new beat
speak of such truths
such that we'd repeat

the message of fairness
our principles of faith

our belief in the doctrine
that once guided our place

the position we had once
As we were so admired
this community here
to which others aspired

Then with a flutter
With a deep dark flash
Wings black and blue
It arrived in a dash

Setting down,
And boldly settling in
It spoke then, demanding
'Why such a din?'

'You've disturbed my mate
You've unsettled our nest
I'm here maybe to help
And not as a pest

The others were becalmed
Sat back, quite relaxed
A turtle showed up
To join in the task

Of trying to determine
Of trying to find
A brilliant solution
A meeting of the mind

So the green feathered frog
And the blue spangled bird
Joined with the others
All clamouring to be heard

But through gentle persuasion,
Some cajoling too
Some answers were settled
Listing what they might do

And as the sun settled down
To frame the dark pond
They all finally agreed
To a plan...to move on

rollercoaster

Up
Down
Sideways, sometimes
A wild ride, most always
Demanding, of course
Also expecting
Expecting that,
Because I love you
I'll go along
For the ride
Always

But the downside is
A weariness
That sets in
A fatigue
One hears about
'Metal fatigue'
Can cause
Something to become
Broken
I offer

'Are we broken?'
You ask
'Not yet – I don't think'

Pregnant silence
Follows

'What are you thinking?'
You ask

'Like a roller coaster'
My reply

Your raised eyebrow
Demands clarity

'The downside is,
I lose you….

Upside?
'No more motion sickness'

It's your smile that hurts the most

This Not that.....

This not that
She said
As I watched her
Unravel the
Ball of multi-coloured
Twine

'This, NOT That'
She repeated
For emphasis
We believed

'For this is different
From that.
You do see
that, don't you?'

This, has a quality
A quality of tactility
The feel of soft dove skin
Of soft doe skin
Of soft - softness

'You do see, that
Don't you?'

Mesmerized, we were
Watching as she slithered the
Hanks of wool through
Extended long tapering fingers

Those fingers', thought I
'In my hair, would be
Terribly erotic.'
My hair, as un-tested yarn

In those fingers, trusting
To those hands
Would act/react with all
The electricity she would
Bring to bear

'This, not, that!'
Was a command,
A pronouncement of Belief
Of unchecked fealty

'But', I meekly offered
'What if 'that', is not
Quite enough?'

She sniffed at the
Sheer arrogance of such a Challenge
Her pert pretty nose
Turned even more upwards
Deigned to acknowledge
The sheer perversity
Of my derring-do

'You', she quietly Commanded
'You, are a charlatan,
An unbeliever
Why are you
Here, even?

Shrivelling I shrank
Visibly, and slunk
Away
To a quieter corner
Where my wounded heart
Could think

On that

YOUR LOVE IS SUCH A THIEF

you used to make me laugh
And sometimes even cry
You used to share your stories
To help the time go by

You used me as your confidante
And that was quite okay
You told me stories sad but true
And you'd beg me then to stay

You used to tell me stories
Of conquests and of times
You used your charm and prettiness
Quoting poetry and rhymes

You used to make me laugh
Least that is what it seems
I faked conspiratorially
An interest in your dreams

You used to make me happy
And we didn't even try
We'd just sit beside each other
And watch the day go by

But you never looked so you didn't see
That inside my heart was bending
Feeling like to break and fail
As I knew it soon was ending

You used to make me laugh
And now you make me cry
As your conquests and your stories
Never could explain the 'why'

Have come just too accustomed
To the hurt and all the tears
Will need to live more carefully now
It's not quite as it appears

You could often make me happy
But sometimes you made me sad
Some days were just the best days
I thought I'd ever had

some days were sometimes harder
some days you were all right
i never knew which demons
might show up in your night

you used to make me laugh
i'd wonder at your stories
i'd giggle as you carried on
forgetting all my worries

you used to make me feel so good
you didn't even have to try
but nowadays that caring's gone
I sit here now, and wonder

Why

Think *not* so much

Of the consequence
But more perhaps
Of the acquisition

Achieved, or earned
As a part result
Of a wilful, or willing
Blindness
A reality

Which if acknowledged
In a conscious state
Would render one
Incapable
In a search for
Their resolve

And look now
Again, mayhaps
Forever
Upon the remaining few
The lesser than
Ever
Repositories of
Once
Calming comfort

The racks
The rows
Of purposed paper
Shaped by glittery
Artful covers
Their alluring messages
Designed to beckon
One

To partake
To pursue
The fantasies
Contained therein

Those artifacts
Of other times
Times past and gone
Now
The imprints of
Cares and curiosities

Strategically placed
In public view
Mirrors of frivolity
Of fun, of distraction
Vessels of a kind

Of comfort
But fossils
Of collected
Collective
Memories

That cannot be delivered in
Other forms or formats
Dodo birds they be

Diminishing in their
Presence as they
Lose, with a frightening
Rapidity
Their foothold on
Society

As like
Are libraries

With an uncertain future
Whose point
And whose purpose may well
Become that they
Maintain their cultural
Value

Not as organs of a
Centered purpose but as
Temples, tributes
Of what once was
Not of what
Might have been

For as we wither
And as we do so
Like an ebbing toothache
We see,
Do we not
On a rocky shore

That little house
Egg creme yellow
Framed in
Ketchup red
But more lively
As it needs to be

And the soldier who sits
On a rickety
Pressed back chair
Atilt against the onslaught
His healthy unhealthy
Hair, yellow silver
Strands
That frame a rodent face

Sitting
Amidst a mirth
Of his very own
Construct
The revolution
Like none other
Has taken control
And even
All
The wise men
Saw not its arrival
Saw not even
Its import

As we, as most
Of us, bereft in our
Loss of livelihood
Are left to
Ponder
What
Next
May befall us?

Who will sound
The alarm?

whisperings

One foot
Placed carefully in front of the other
Balance, elusive
As I stay within the cover

Embraced by murky darkness
As I seek to find my way
As snow drifts almost
Invisibly

And yet, stopping to catch my breath
With a sigh
I turn my face upwards
Seeing nothing
Really
Yet feeling
Angel's teardrops
As they whisper against my face

Cooling me
Tempering my
Temperature
Cooling but not
Calming
Me

Pause…more, pause
To continue?
Is this just silly?
The question bubbles
Against my heart
Which is frail
Now

Perhaps

Turn back
Do not persist
Do not pursue
Fall amidst
A drift
So alluring

So alluring
Like you

Just
Like you

And yet

And yet
There is a need
To know
A need to confront
Even if it finds
Sorrow

And pain

And so
I wait
Waiting for another breath
To propel me now
And next
Across the open field
To home

Sweat beads against
My brow
As I push away
As I go
Now

Slipping silently
Seen by only snow
Drops
Dripping
As they do
Against my fever
As I know
I seek
you

Hoping to find
Only you
There

Silent approach,
Knees each held high
To clear the drifts

No sound
At all
Not a sigh

As with relief I find
And fall
Aside the window
Open slightly
For as i recall

That is the way
You like it

Slumped and slouched
Back against the wall
Waiting in gloomy
Silence

For what?

I'm not sure
Not at all
Sure

But hope rides above
Any pent up emotions
Against each and every notion
That you are

Not alone

I wait
In soft silence
Almost hearing the fine
snowdrops
As they kiss the drifts about

I wait
For some quite
Long time
Arriving finally at a
Safer place
I hope

Until

Until a whisper slips
Across the window frame
'no'

I hear
'no'. .again
Then

'yes'

'Yes'

Framed in a more
Urgent whisper

And then
And then

I hear only

My heart breaking

timeXdistance

Oh!
How is it
We've aged
And
How have we
Gauged
The distance
And difference
And the time
In between
Us?

Are we sepia-toned
Cold blue,
To the bone
Tried
Sometimes to be true
To
Only ourselves?

Or black-white
As in which
Should come
First
In order
Of choice
Or in order
Of consequence

How is it we've
Aged
And how have we
Staged
A threshold
Of chapters

Each Unto
Itself?

Where have we
Been
And where have we
Gone
And did we come back
Or did we carry on

And to where
And to what
Did we maybe satisfy
An aim, an idea
Or was it simply,
And only
Just a
Mystery

Yet time has
Become
Distance
And dash
And the difference
Quite simply
Lies in a brash
And simply
Unordinary
Debate and decline
To the question
Throughout
Your, and my
Time
Does it matter
A whit
Or matter
A bit

Of dust and confusion
Sorting through It

Or black-white
As in which
Should be first
Are our actions honest
Or simply rehearsed?

To find there
A truth
Not wanting
To be found
Thus this distance
Or difference
Goes round, goes round

To the point where
Both lines and
Memories collide
As we stealthily
Seek what we
Now see is outside

Of the time
And the distance
And the engulfing
Years
And all that time wasted
Washed away
In our tears

To a time which
Is captured
Now here in this day
Allowing me finally
To stand up and say

How is it
We've aged
And
How have we
Gauged
The distance
And difference
And the time
In between
                                        Us

isolation

I
solation

solitary

and alone

thoughts, ideas – desires

wishes, hopes, dreams

ever an aloneness

little changes

it seems

silence

in a vacuum

is noisier

than

the silence in my head

questions persist

answers rarely arise

out of the bleak

landscape

of our lives

time trickles

meanders like my thoughts

to return to tomorrow

a

s3ns3

of serenity, forced

exists

in this compound

of hermitage

courage continues

to persuade me

to continue this difficult

quest toward normality

in this cocoon of silent

embrace

where arguments are

watched but

unheard

as day devolves to day

week to month

time trickles sadly

ahead

and one fulsome fear

forcibly it would appear

to join those others close

to death and dying

in such a place of

hopeful care

and the crying

heard about

would be in part

my own

for to face death

there in that place

without those loves about

restricted to

solitary confinement

confined to die

alone

and wanting

only to see, once again

Those loves

FAR PAINTED FADED HILLS

Far painted faded hills
A purpley-blue twilight
Pulling at my senses
Tug me out into the night

Roads, soft, cut like ribbons
Through high towering trees
Leading paths go onwards
To outward rushing seas

The call upon my nerve ends
Which just quite won't abate
Demands of me obedience
Before it's all too late

Night skies black and chill winds
That cut to, through the bone
Demand of me attention
Won't leave me here alone

Paths in falling trickles
Down and to the right
A deeper glen is calling
Me out into the night

Dark stream that flashes bubbles
Embracing to the stones
Beckons me seductively
In soft and pearly tones

And the road that outward winds
Past tomorrows' distant dawn
Still tolerates no bargaining
Demands that, I just carry on

In the dark

Does it thrive?
Does it come
To life?

Like rats that
Scurry
About
Fearless
Feared
Bold

Braced by certainty
Of
Possession

And the rights of

Dominion
As night creeps
So come
The creeps

Crawling from and to
Rocks, foundations

They slither, eyes front
Eyes to the rear
Not to see
Where they've been
But to see who might be
Following

For fear
If addressed by any sense
Of honesty

Fear is the being caught
Not a fear of doing
What they do

Scars
Are the currency
Of
Their artistry

Blemishes are
Weak, half-hearted
Pothos
Heart-shaped
Evil grows
In darker light

Thriving against
the dark chasms
the secret, hidden
valleys
of their endeavours

unseen
and therefore
unimpeded in their dash
to urgent completion
of misguided tasks
that celebrate

oblivion

these rats of the night
armed by aerosol
but lacking both
moral certitude
or pride of place

they work solely
to deface
that which is not
theirs

and the words
of their meanings
'Trasc'
'Escape'
'xPass'

but nary a
passage
intent to
disarm
intent to
destroy
tranquility

a need to impose
on those who have
no interest
on those who will not
offer, provide
any hope for their
warped endeavours

sitting
watching
wary
warily
in this dark place
seeking to see
the efforts underway
in that dark space

Pothos

persists
prevails in spite of
danger signs
signals of
human nature

the call of
human consideration
this callous
indifference
to values other than
their own

and in their owning
with the beigerence
of indifference
they continue
unchecked
unabated

for we
the citizens who have
earned the right
who have paid
for the right(s)
of expectation
of courtesy
and of
respect

do little
do nothing
to prevent
to provide
barricades to
such arrogant
and such ignorant

purpose(s)

shameful
that we
who have earned the right
of custodianship
who have earned the
responsibility
of responsibility

shameful
that we
en masse
do not
cannot
have not
the courage of
convictions
that are passed on
to us
to stand in the
glow of
our own defiance
to proclaim
our rights of
earned and paid for
expectation

of the visible serenity
of this
our environment

no

not their environment
although they would
have us think

believe

otherwise

why?

and where is the promised
fortitude of
capture and
confrontation
where is the promised
fortitude of
commitment to

equitability?

it is, it has been
wrest from us

                              alas!

Bleaker Street

Bleak
The streets
Are running black with rain

Twisting rivulets
Slide
Circling a drain

Rubbery licorice
Like plastic misshapen
Contours of life
Slipping away

These days dark
Not ending 'till night
Blessedly for some
Comes

Gloom pervades
Persistently permeates
Our streets today
Cedars sway, they grace
Tree trunks glistening
Society's tears sliding
In downward spirals

Watches, clocks - time
Has become a fluid course
Of tolerance
Waning patients
For better or worse

Lives unravel
Children's cries, cry out
Mothers arms, wearier
now

As patience demands
An end

rectitude

The night rose
Like a dark surprise
From beyond the
Far hedges
That formed and framed
The place in which
I found myself

Awake

Like tricky pearls
Their luminescence
Served as a fraudulent
Reminder of
Truths
And of
Some lies

I waited
I waited
For oh so long
So painfully long
To hear
The waterdrop
As it filtered through
Balsa leaves
Delicate
Like I had
Become

The night
Which had been once
My friend
Betrayed me
With false promises

Seduced me with
Other
Promises

Left me bereft
Bereft
Alone
The dark of the
Crystal
Membrane of memory
The murk of
Distant remembrances

Shattering, shuttered
Shattered the little
corner
Of my soul that
Once upon a time
I had
Promised to you

And as I
Revi/ew
This dark place
Where I search still
For you

I find a vacuum only
Where life
And the promise of
Living wider
Bolder
braver

once resided and
resonated
with a pulse

with the promise of
more

but, more or
less
lesser than
is the residue
that slides against
the dew
of this day's
dawn

as
with a sigh
I turn,
Knowing I will
Find you

Gone

And with spirit
Still a part of my
Resolve
I venture forth

Against the nightclouds
Unafraid
In my solitariness
Comforted by the
Faith that

A day will yet come
When I might place
Upon your soul

Those very pearls

Forsooth

night·stockings

night stockings
play dark
their fibres rough

glassine frames
of brittle memories
spread across

grassy seas
to ebb, to flow
against sliding, winding
currents

windmill blades
broke
splintered along
the lines of
edgy memories
times left behind

rippling eddies
that swell
blistering under
a hot moonlight

the watchmen
go through the motions

of paying attention
measuring tension

wearily waiting
for the other
Dawn

when it arrives
pulls into a
reluctant station
amid shouts and cries
trumpeted gestations

morbid gesticulations

can't possibly

save this day

bedskIrts

and the light slipped, silently
across the old floorboards.
It crept along the base of the wall
seeming to pause at the bottom of the bedskirt

As if thinking, as if contemplating its course,
a graceful rest for a gracious moment -
it lingered, then stole, determinedly,
up through the folds of fabric
to the very crest of the
mattress upon which she lay

As if possessed of a living lifeform,
it surrendered once again to the moment -
to the quietude, the solemnity
of the special space to which it had come

As if with sight, as if with eyes, as if with ears,
the soft breathing was seen, was felt -
was washing through and around
a cocoon of enveloping body heat

And as if it might be measured,
the heat was becoming warmth,
the heat was becoming cool
the heat was leaving, quietly,
the frame and the form,
of her.

For such time had come,
such time such that she now knew,
the sadness of loss that had become her
compass,
was all that she had left to her,
of him

And so it was that with a little catch
as a murmur in her throat,
as the quivering pulse of her life,
fell to pieces, fell away from her,
she had one sense left of which was hers
and hers alone   regret.

pandemicPoem

As I look out this porthole of this alien place
I see the mist, the rain - the clouds and vapour - drift across
the plane of reality.

Although the barren trees sway their blank branches,
stick-like tentacles reaching,
seeking a higher power -
I watch as the miasma of fear and doubt
tighten their grip

on our world

on this landscape of misery

Fading light frames the limits of my rectilinear horizon
a box of a viewpoint
shaped and shuttered
by the events of recent yesterdays

there is a pain a deep and penetrative pain
that has lodged in my chest
as I look - as I hope

to find some form of indication '
that there is
that there may be a roadmap
out of and away from
these desolate shores
feeling bleak and feeling forlorn

Hoping to find, to stumble across
a flicker of light,
a shard of optimistic faith and belief,
I sit and watch the wash and wavering

Of this wind of death and completion
If this world is to acknowledge its defeat at
the ends of ineptitude, if this world is to give up its grace and soul - to these invaders

If this world that we have known, have loved - have abused and rejected
Is to recover - ever to recover - it will not be for reasons of promise
It will be for reasons of determined execution

Pray that may not be ours

s i l e n z i o

This silence is worse
By far
Than the noise

The blackness is worse
By far
Than the light

The tone and the tenor
Of loud thoughts
They cocoon the senses
Like quiet thieves

They ease in
Unseen
Into and about
The night

Tremors and terrors
Unacknowledged
Purposefully
Or with deliberation

The twists, the turns
Of misty, messy memories
Of times, good times
And of bad

Such that now,
Such that here
I look at you
I see you
I know,
How you are now, sad

And the silence is worse
By far
Than the noise

For the noise
Painful as it was
Served to tell me
You were   Still here

ALONE

Are you alone?

Yes

Are you afraid?

Yes

What are you afraid of?

I don't know – I'm just, frightened and afraid

Did someone hurt you?

Yes

How?

By lying to me

By lying to you?

Yes

And this lie….it was an important thing?

Yes

Can you tell me?

I can, but, I can't

And why not?

Because it hurts, too, much

What do you think might happen if you were to tell me?

I'm not sure – but I know, it will hurt again, even more

Okay. Can I help you? Somehow?

Maybe – maybe. Can you make the pain go away?

Perhaps – I have ways

Will you tell me? Show me?

I'm not sure. It may hurt you more

Why?

Sometimes the remedy is more painful than the cure
Sometimes the remedy is more costly than one can afford
Why are you alone? Can you tell me that?

No – yes, but no

Does no one care for you, about you?

I don't think so

Was there ever anyone who cared for you, about you?

Yes

What happened to them?

I lost – them

How?

From fear. I lost them from fear. Or because of fear.

Do you still have that fear?

Yes.

Can you be strong?

I don't know

Can you be stronger than the fear? If your strength were to help you to
move to a better, stronger place?

I don't know

How might I help?

*Can you just hold me? Just a little. I miss – I miss the hugs, have lost
the comfort of closeness.*

PROSE

Celestial

Dunno....or, don't know........the combination of Francis Cabrel and Gypsy Kings......I feel, wafted.......floating and soaring over lush landscapes, elegant guitar licks popping in my ears.

"La Corrida" sorta sums it up...."Carte Postale" follows on.

I sit, and listen – as the waves break gently on this Adriatic shore.

The wine, is rich, red and full of promise.

As is this day.......

Have little to do – certainly nothing I'm obliged to do.

Unless you count Celeste......that's another matter.

But, for now – I drift and continue to pop and bob, psychically – above the world about

me.

I suppose, at some point – I should meet my obligations......at least those to myself, if

not others.

But – why, frankly....should I bother?

Money – thankfully, is not an issue. It used to be before the Day....but, not now.

Since then, I have marked and measured each day with a grateful sigh and a giddy self-congratulatory swoosh!

And now, "Je t'aimais, je t'aime', je t'aimerai", by Francis Cabrel bursts into my reverie.

Causes me to think, to reflect – back to those others, that I loved, wanted to love…..should have loved.

And, yet – here I am – here…on a pebbled and gnarly beach – alone.

And so, to Celeste….hear me now.

'Je t'aimais, je t'aime je t'aimerai' – is, and was, and will be – my message to you…… to what might have, or should – have been.

Cold Ottawa nights, warmed by Montreal joie de vivre……and quebecois passion……it amounts, to far more than I ever could.

This night, here….warm – against the gentle stones of a distant beach, might want to trade itself for the warmth of toe-tingling passion in an embrace of you……

Is there any way that I could find a return path to that point, that time – that passion that propelled you to me….and which ricocheted off and away from my feeble heart?

Is that a question? Or, is that a question that requires or deserves, an answer?

Dunno – that again….but true, as it is.

I may, I might – wait here. There is nowhere else I want to go……my accommodation is secure and guaranteed…..there is no one to be accountable to, but to you.

And you – are far too far away from here……so, this bottle of rich red will suffice to comfort me into and beyond the night sky. But – I see you….there. Alone (hopefully) as I am. And I surrender to the question, 'Why did it come to this?'

Well, we both know – or think we know. A dark, and a cold night – as we drove along the coast…..you, snuggled closer to me than safe – me, aroused by the wetness on your inner thigh, the catch in your voice as you asked, 'How much further?'

And my answer, gave no value…..

And so – we drove, on and into the night. Both, I'm sure with fragments/figments of fiery imagination – as to where we might arrive, when, and what it might all come to……

Domeni

It was a day of immense, intense excitement and anticipation

A day of the **Annual Event** - the morning he and the others had patiently, and impatiently, awaited.

It was the culmination - then of a weary and depressing road of self deprivation as they had schemed, connived and cleverly sought to contrive the sleekest, slickest plan to ensure that they were the first - the very most first, ones in line when the doors opened at 7:00 AM sharp.

Of course they were well prepared, thoroughly rehearsed - smooth in their talking techniques…..they had, he was sure, anticipated every possible instance of what might go wrong.

A year! A whole year they had plotted, saved and slaved to reach this point - and, as is it was the custom, it could only be - would only be, this year. For the day after tomorrow they would have all passed through the rigorous ritual of rights - to be no longer ever qualified to have a second chance should they fail.

Being the leader, that burden fell to him to carefully explain, to devise - to strategize their plan.

And now, a scant two hours before they were due to present themselves, it was time to gather their packs, retrieve their hidden currency, bundle themselves against the frigid bitter cold, wrap thick woolen scarves about their heads, ears and necks and set off.

Him, in the lead.

The other, typically would follow in single file.

But that part was not written - not written like all other elements of the ritual requirements.

If Berkely wished to stride alongside him for a piece, chattering about his plan once admitted, well - that was okay.

Being the leader he had gained a modicum of elegant reserve - such that his mere attitude, or downwards glance across the bridge of his overly high nose, might convey command.

Or, if Hyacinth, her burnished and coiled red, coppery hair spraying out from under the brightly patterned headscarf as like beacon in that early morning gloom - if Hyacinth were to slide closer to him and with a warm toffee-like smile, ask him is he was truly now excited.

Regardless, he would without breaking stride push on over the snow-packed roadway, allowing himself to get lost in a mindless fascination for the odd-shaped and infinite number of size, shapes and form of the big snow puffballs that lined the side of the road.

Their boots squeaked against the rigid packed snow. His grandfather had always warned him - 'When you hear yer boots a squeakin' against the road snow - ya knows it's probably ne'er been quite this cold.'

There was no stopping - none. Not for needs of any kind - be it pain, toilet or cold. There existed only a crisp straight line from their starting out point and their destination.

If one tired, got sick, was too fatigued they were simply left behind. It was understood that they had abandoned any right to continue, to catch up. Their only option was to, in a sense of humbling shame, turn about and return to face derision and embarrassment by the others.

As the hour moved on both Hyacinth and Berkely dropped back - back into single file. If anything his strength blossomed - he stepped more lively, carried by the dawning exultation of a successful arrival, a triumphant achievement.

And then, the last curve in the roadway before turning into the downslope that led to the village square.

All clouds had drifted off, slipped apart to leave the sharp white light of the moon focused, it seemed, on only the centre of the square.

At that point he raised his hand for all to stop. They did and slowly drifted up to stand alongside of him.

Inhaling deeply, raising his eyes to the moon, and with a slow exhale he said softly, but clearly, "We are now where we have always been intended to be. A few more moments and we will stand, as soldiers, in a strict straight line, facing the portal - which will open to great and welcome us on this momentous morn. Are we ready, all?', he asked.

No words - not a sound. Only a solemn bowing of every head, momentarily - and then as he set off to descend the rise towards the square they fell in, again, behind in a straight but proud line.

Arriving at the bordered edge of the square, he took up position directly in front of the heavy carved oak doors, their brass handles and hardware shining like gold in the moonlight.

They stood, rigidly, neither talking or glancing about. Not curious or concerned about others who drifted into the square, some to fall into line behind them.

Time passed like treacly molasses. Most others might well have fidgeted and fussed. Not they.

And in time, with a coarse sound of a heavy weight being dragged, the large double doors opened wide.

A golden light flowed, like a river, outwards to grace and to bathe them in a suggestion of warmth and welcome.

Shortly, one of authority seemed to appear to the right of the doors. Raising a scroll to eye level, the voice began, 'Jason, Rebecca, Berkely, Hyacinth - and on until twenty-one names had been called.

As each name rang out the line moved forward in a measured step.

Upon the twenty-first that passed through and into the large stone arch, the doors began a slow and silent closing.

A wail went up from all those who had not gained entry.

The scribe, once the doors were again shut, dark and silent, turned to the assembled remains, announcing, 'We are, for this year, this season, done now once again'

'You may leave and find your ways about your lives and purpose.'

Anno domini sequen tal

Bereshith
In the beginning

And from the darkness sprang life. In the most feeble and fragile of form.

Life, endured – as if by design, as it was always intended to.

In the course of life – in and through the course of my life, darkness was never to be feared. Nor did it imbue in me fearfulness. The gathering shadows, as they descend about us, as night falls towards another day, a growing dawn.

Perhaps in my youth, as a young newspaper delivery boy, I strode through such darkness as I fulfilled my responsibilities – timely deliveries.

Solitude, became to me, a friend. It was always a constant, shifting and changing according to atmospheric negotiations – but never in such a way that it frightened me.

The following years flowed, as I was propelled along paths and over horizons to discover all the worlds that touched on my life, my living. Always it seems that the coming of night was synonymous with a blanket of comfort. It was, always, an enjoyable refuge.

A growing awareness began to develop in my day to day journey. At a certain age – which I can not accurately recall – my daily dawn would coax me into early morning consciousness at, what seemed like ridiculously early hours.

Four A.M. seemed to be, and still is, the most constant. Although whatever is the master of my universe it will occasionally trip me up, calling on me to become awake once more at 3:00 o'clock – or at other odd hours.

Coming to recognize the futility of argument the late night shroud of darkness would push me to get up – arise – get on with productive endeavors. And in those times, when I was curiously convinced, that there was no one up and awake but me, I came to find a warmth – a warmth of familiarity in the comfort of constancy.

Until.

Until the world tilted, sideways. Or perhaps upside down. Impossible really to discern in the dark, for the normal visual frames of reference are understandably obscured.

Those late-night-early- mornings became anxiety riddled, as I and the rest of the world became aware of an approaching horror. In the same way that one, is generally unaware of an approaching tsunami. In our uninformed ignorance, we don't see it – we don't hear it. We feel it only when and as it crashes against, around and through our lives.

Such were the crushing currents that conspired to tilt our world, to exacerbate the wobble on its axis, as reports – faint at first – of odd life forms, deep dark caves, filtered into our early mornings. And came, all too quickly, to fill our days.

Fear, then changed. It changed, morphed into that most fearful states – fear of the unknown.

And blacks became blacker. Nights became both vicious and unforgiving, as the dying and the dead reset the compass of our lives.

Through the static of mis-direction, of lies and untruths, we awoke into a different darkness – one in which light seemed to all but disappear.

Valiant efforts, brave initiatives rose up to fight, do battle – engage the beast, vanquish the devil. Some have had, some success. Others, like vapors set in fantasy, have served only to provide a fleeting glimmer of hope.

And thus it has been. Bereshith.

Tsum suf, 'at the end' — is written in an inky black script on a midnight black background, perhaps as a sad prophecy.

But as I gaze out into the void, across to the far horizon, the spark I see there on the very rim, has me asking,

'Might that be, the light of reason?'

Where Do You Put It?

His heart was loudly beating, it was tightening up, his breath, seizing. He was trying to grasp a normal breath, as he approached.

Beyond frightened, afraid of ridicule, terrified of humiliating rejection he steeled himself.

She sat poised at a library table - part of her beauty, that intrinsic ethereal halo that embraced her, was that she had no idea, that she sat, poised….

'How uniquely beautiful', he caught himself thinking.

She was, absorbed in the papers she was reading.

He turned away….a sudden complete 180 degree turn.

'Need to breathe….need to breathe', pounded through his head.

After struggling to reach the zen-like state that he had been practising, he drew himself up, once more. With a steely resolve, he turned back, his sweaty palms gripping the yellow rose he had brought. For her.

She was gone!

How could she be gone? She was just there……'Oh God!', 'I can't ever do this again -to find find the courage….'

Eyes smarting with tears and angry at himself, his cowardice….. his fears

he stepped to the side, leaning himself - propping himself up against the end of the stacks……

'Hey! Careful there….'

He turned quickly.

There - there she was, standing, pencil clamped between her teeth, a raft of papers in one hand and an open book in the other….

….and wrapped about the pencil, the blossoming of a smile.

And the eyes, violet, sparking……

'OhMYGod!', he blurted out. He thought he had burbled it inside his swelling brain.

But no….

Immediately concerned she took the pencil from between her teeth, reached out to steady him.

'Are you okay", she asked?

From somewhere, from some place way deep inside, he knew this was the moment.

He straightened - pulled himself more upright. Found a smile and watched it drift towards her.

'Yes, yes…sorry. Sorry to disturb you.'

'No - it's okay', she said, reaching out with a helping hand.

'But, but – and I'm sorry - I have a question for you', extending the yellow rose towards her…….

Completely baffled, confused, she looked into his eyes, while tentatively reaching for the sunshine of the flower….

'Yes, of course, what is it?', she asked with the whisper of a smile. 'Did you want to ask me something?'

'I did - I mean I do...... and I apologize for intruding. As I have noticed you these past weeks, around campus, I have been meaning to ask you this....'

He took a deep breath releasing the rose into her hand. 'Where do you put it?'

Puzzled and slightly uncertain, she stared at him.

'Put what?'

'My breath', he replied, the rush of words tumbling from him. 'Where do you put my breath?' Feeling out of control, he rushed, 'Cause every time I see you, you take my breath away......and I wander aimlessly about, wondering, 'When will I see her again, and will she ever give it back - to me?'

A radiance exploded into a dazzling smile.

'How ever so sweet!', she said.

She glanced down towards the floor, then raised her head to look, laser-like into his eyes.

He was now, holding his breath – waiting.

'Tell you what... Let me think on that and I'll try to give you an answer the next time we get together.'

He smiled hesitatingly, sweating – hopeful, uncertain. His hands, clammy, his eyes felt like an unwelcome grit had settled there.

He watched, tense, fearful as she raised her gaze from the floor to look directly at him.

Then gently and softly, smiling like a sunbeam through the treetops, she paused, then said, 'There will be a next time won't there?'

My Spooky Friends

Dean, Kirk, Ralph and the Bear….

Dean in a dinner jacket, tie askew, slim, elegant – martini glass in hand

Kirk - urbane, hair slightly longer than the fashion, over curling his powder blue button down shirt - cigarette smoke drifting halo-like, eyes heavy lidded, looking down at the half-empty scotch glass

Ralph, rough, raggedy - cowboy hat askew - unshaven, cigar gripped between his teeth, eyes squinting from the smoke - a fistful of cards, eying the pot in the centre of the table…..

and the 'Bear - his navy blue double-breasted blazer casually open, cigarette dangling from the corner of his mouth - a cold beer, rivulets running down the sides of the glass……his goatee trimmed to the max…..leaning back in his chair, watching - waiting

Gathered around the poker table, a tin-hooded light suspended over the centre - a foot beyond the edge of the table was pitch blackness…..one sensed body heat out there, felt the rustle of satin against lace….

The rain splattered timpani-like against the old wood framed window panes.

Somewhere - from the deep darkness beyond, guitar riffs played against the slip and slide of piano notes.

'So - you in, you not in?', Kirk asked.

The Bear smiled, flicked the ash of his cigarette into the dead centre of the ashtray

These are - these **were,** my friends….all dead now, sadly. Not seemingly sadly for them though…….they are where they were most comfortable, some crispy/crunchy log cabin in the Hampshires or Muskoka. Probably a Tuesday night. For them, time, dates, when, - made no difference, dead as they were.

They visited me, occasionally. Of late, more frequently. Which was becoming a little more than mildly concerning as I had heard from others, former friends, who came to call, that as the frequency of such visitations increased so did, in direct proportion, the timeframe left available to them, those here, alive and living.

But, I did truly miss them. All of them. Though none of them had met one another before their deaths, they had become, it seems, to one another, a closed caption of comfortable friends.

But, I had work to get out that night and I would have to wait 'till my next visit to see how all the betting played out.

'So - whaddaya think? Should we….?'

'Nah. Don't think so - too risky. But we can 'listen in'- maybe contrive to help out in some small way.

That was Dean and Kirk in conversation. After the poker game wrapped up, lights were turned out and they were sitting out on the verandah under the fluted metal roofing, each with a smidgen of cognac still in their glass.

Rain had mostly stopped. The occasional dripDrip hit the awning above them and trickled down to the decking.

'It's too early', Kirk said, 'We don't want to spook him….'

'Hah! Funny one,' replied Dean. 'Spook him - guess that's what a normal mortal would think, yeah.?'

'Well we do be spooks, we do be.' Kirk replied.

under Observation

Kevin.
What can be said about Kevin? Shrewd, certainly.

Astute - clever......some, those who have been in competition with Kevin would probably say, begrudgingly - brilliant. That may all be true. But, Kevin had other talents - hidden assets you might say. Given time and opportunity - and the proper alignment of heavenly bodies, you might discover those talents - or some of them. And in the process, secrets. Very good at secrets Kevin was.....mostly secrets of a most personal nature. See.....Kevin was gay, but you would never know it by looking at her.

By all accounts, happily immersed in a robust relationship, for some years, the obvious conclusion would be that Kevin was very sexually active, probably erotically adventurous, and most likely indefatigable in terms of efforts and ardor. Certainly none of her frequent engagements played out across the city would contradict that presumption.

Emilio
Emilio, on the other hand, was - of the other hand. In that he was in most all things left-handed - except for masturbation. By some quirk of psycho-sexual compass bearing, in that act, he could only achieve orgasm using his right hand. Needs a lot more study.....

Teresa.
And then there was Teresa. Ahhhhh....Teresa. A heavenly body if ever there was one. Tall, lithe, supple, high-breasted. High intellect. She could argue pro or con within seconds of either position and walk away having convinced the sparring partner that her argument was in fact the only argument. That was what made her such a great ...... cleaning lady.

Caprice
But Caprice - well, she was neither up to her namesake - not capricious or adventurous. But with an eye, and more importantly, a sense for figures and numbers, there was no one who could present a financial analysis or as thorough a model projection, as Caprice. She was solid, thorough and ever industrious.

Harvey
Harvey though was a renegade. At least in his mind. But truthfully, isn't that what really counts? Not just the perception of one's self, but the ability, the determination to act on that perception. He thought often to himself, 'You are what you say you are!' And in demonstrable fashion challenged anyone, to challenge him. With such a firm cornerstone of character he had managed to rise above most all the other executives in the partnership to sit there, in a position of power, which based solely on an analysis of his educational

merit, would normally never have happened. Yet, there he was. Brash, bold, brazen - unafraid to tackle any challenge.

Ulla

Ulla though was decidedly different. Slight and slender, wiry one might say, she looked to be a competitive gymnast. But one always had the uneasy feeling that in the deep pools of char-brown eyes, there lurked a viciousness. And you would be right. She, and only she, could claim - and prove if needed, that she had put down many a foe. Permanently. Like as in forever. Like forever dead. Her quiet and intense demeanour hid the ferocious tenacity that was instantly on call when she so needed it. Either for her own benefit or pursuit - or in support of one of the many assignments she carried out for the organization.

Heinz was mulling all this over as he absently stood in line in the hospital cafeteria, waiting to order yet another fast food lunch so that he could rush back to his office to meet the next patient.

All these personas, he was thinking. All the personalities and personality disorders. How best to serve the patient, that was always the centre of his practise and his professional compass.

Pierrette suddenly popped into his mind. 'Ah, Pierette.....the lovely Pierette'. He admonished himself, sternly, for even allowing such a fanciful feeling to blossom. And, she did need his help. Probably more that the others he had been thinking about. 'I must find a way to let her find a way to some form of comfort. A way out of the turmoil of her psyche. Maybe, if I could….'

He was abruptly brought back to the present when the server behind the counter demanded of him, 'Good day Doctor…..Would you like ketchup with those fries?'

The only response that immediately sprung to mind was 'Not on your life. I've had far more than enough already.' the last said with a bit of a suppressed giggle. 'Imagine', he thought. 'If my colleagues really knew what went on in my head…..'

'No problem….how about some 57 sauce then?'

'Now THAT might be interesting', he replied.

'Hmmmmm! Interesting indeed…… there's 7 of them already living in his head. Might there be another 50?' he mused. Requires more study' as he threaded through the tables to a far corner where he could be again, alone with his thoughts and all

of their friends. Defintely, more study. He giggled. Again.

BUBBLES.

She awoke to bubbles.

Tickles and giggles and bubbles and bursts of frenzied fizzy feelings. As if she was about to pop right out of her skin. The tingles touched her smile and drew it- wider.-She was breathless, flushed, and fevered.

Sometimes when flying, and she tapped down on the left rudder pedal and pulled the yoke to port, the plane would sideslip, its left wing would dip towards the earth – and for a moment it was that intense sensation of the bottom dropping out of the world. That was similar, but not as intense as what she was feeling at the moment.

She dropped her hands to her sides, lying flat on her back, staring up at the ceiling.

'Hang on, cherie', she muttered. 'Hang on!'

He was coming to see her – he was coming back. She had resigned herself to their choice. She'd recovered her old self. She was able to sit in meetings, direct her team, find inspiration for new and wonderful concepts. She had finally rediscovered the deep well of her natural born talents.

It had been tough. It had been brutal, painful, sad beyond tears. And now that time had put the tears behind her she felt whole and vital once again. She knew they might re-build their fairy tale.

Closing her eyes she allowed her mind to drift, as on a wave of alka-seltzer froth. It was a year since that first encounter. Sitting completely engrossed in a presentation she was reviewing at a table in Starbucks, she was suddenly jostled from behind.

Her chair, bumped forward, had pulled her from her concentration. She had half turned in her seat to see what was happening, when she looked up into his green eyes.

'I'm so very sorry, ma' am. Didn't mean to disturb you. I was just trying to plug my phone in here.' He pointed to the wall outlet.

Her immediate reaction had been to flare up at the abrupt intrusion, but the power of his eyes, and the embarrassed half-smile that played at the corners of his mouth, stopped the words. She, unexpectedly, felt a flush of embarrassment. The cultured British accent erased any lingering sense of annoyance.

She rested her arm on the back of the bentwood chair, half turned towards him. And in that glance she was aware of numerous things that pulled at her attention. She registered the bottle-green corduroy pants, and the soft rust coloured suede jacket.

His shirt, a fine tattersal check, of a soft flannel, was a perfect counter-point.

'Perfectly okay,' she said, gazing up at him. His hair, somewhat longish, with a natural wave in it, was lustrous and full—a little over his ears giving him a roguish look.

She wanted to talk more, but her cell-phone rang. Reflexively she looked at the phone, to see who was calling. She had to answer.

Still looking up at him, she fumbled the phone up off the table, and with her eyes and a hand motion to him indicated she had no choice but to take the call.

He smiled, a dazzling smile, and mouthed, 'It's okay – again, very sorry', and waved gently to her as he turned to sit at his own table.

Somewhat exasperatedly she punched the answer button, and said, 'Oui – hello. This is Chantal.'

'Salut cherie', she heard. 'Where are you?'

'Hi Jason. I'm actually at a Starbucks – trying to fine-tune our presentation. And you?'

'I'm downtown about a block from our appointment. Yeah – I know, I'm always the overly early bird. But, didn't know what to expect with traffic, and downtown Miami can be difficult at the best of times. So, I'm going to find a Starbucks or something also. How long will you be? We have a little over an hour before our meeting.'

'Well, I'm just over in South Beach. Can be there in 15 minutes. Give me half an hour to finish this up and I'll meet you in the lobby of the building there.'

'Sounds good', he said. 'Ciao', and he rang off.

She turned around to say something to the English gentleman, and was instantly disappointed to find him in earnest conversation with a beautiful blonde woman. She was a knockout in a bikini that was clearly visible under the gauzy wrap she had tied about herself.

She would have liked to have had the chance to speak with him. At least to introduce herself.

She turned her attention back to her laptop and for the next several minutes was completely caught up in the presentation document.

Checking her watch she found that over twenty minutes had flashed by. Realising she still had to pay her bill, pack up, and find a cab, she started to shut down her computer.

She turned in her chair to retrieve her portfolio case, and also realized that Mr Britain was no longer at the table. Nor was his accomplice. She knew that one of her great assets, as well as a sometimes negative, was her ability to completely immerse herself in a task at hand and be unawares of what went on around her.

But she also felt a little let down, again. She would have liked a shot of his charm.

She stood and organized all her things on a chair and walked over to the cash to settle her bill.

A tall, lanky barista, at the cash, watched her as she approached. As she placed her wallet on the counter he held up one hand imperiously.

'No!' he said. 'Senor has taken care of the lovely lady. And he asked me to give you this....' And he extended a business card towards her.

'I think he left a note for you on the back. Such a sweet man – too bad he's chasing you and not me,' he said with the flash of a grin and a toss of his ponytail.

'Oh,' she stuttered. 'That was very kind of him. I didn't see him leave...'

'It's no a matter', he said. 'Buena suerte en el amor. Good luck in love.'

She smiled, and looked at the card.

Daniel Heath-Jones
Director, International Relations Public Affairs
The London News Network

She turned the card over and read 'So very sorry once again. Perhaps we might have a proper coffee, or tea, together? You can contact me at 615-220-1221. Daniel'

Bubbles..... the sense of bubbles skittering about in her stomach and up into her chest brought a broad smile to her face.

Looking up at the barista, she said, 'Mucho gracias, senor.' She turned, gathered up her things and strode towards the front door..

That, she recalled, was the beginning. And it was followed by months of an emotional madness she had never before experienced. A tempestuous relationship that ultimately failed in crushing pain and recriminations - and her blind determination to find her balance again.   And as memories and images slipped through her mind, she rode the roller coaster of those days and nights as they swung her up, down, sideways – side-slipping, almost delirious at times with happiness.

'Tonight!' she promised silently. 'Tonight....we'll make it all better. We'll make it all good again. We'll cross that bridge and together, explore the mysteries of our future.'

With that she got up from her bed, padded across the polished concrete floor and pulled open the gauzy sheers that covered the floor-to-ceiling windows.

The day was crisp clear and full of the promise she felt inside.

MOLLY MABES

The diner counter ran in an elongated u-shape from the open kitchen window parallel to the entrance door.

She sat there idly twirling the spoon in the chipped enamel coffee mug.

To her right the front of the old place was framed with a series of paned windows that ran from the tabletop all the way up to the vaulted ceiling. Behind her, beyond a trellised screen, was a series of tables and chairs. That section could accommodate 24 by code - but on a busy Friday night in a cold December, that section would be overrun with the various locals and their friends, and sometimes their families.

Every few seconds or so the spoon clicked against the sides of the mug.

'Mabes! Shut the fuck up, okay?', came an impatient growl from just down the counter a ways. 'You're annoying the shit outta me. Can't focus to read the fucking paper.'

Her eyes drifted up from the scarred laminate countertop, dipped into a kind of focus as she swivelled to look to the right.

'Josie, you cain't fucking read anyways - who you kidding?'

'Just stop the infernal spoon rattling - okay?' he replied.

Her gaze moved back to the middle distance resting on the wall opposite. It was a series of barn wood planks nailed horizontally, on which were a series of mis-matched coathooks.

Her shoulders sagged a little as she raised the now cooled-down coffee to her lips.

As she did so a sudden movement on the walkway leading up to the entrance portico caught her attention.

She kinda did a second take for she wasn't exactly seeing what she thought she was seeing. A man was approaching, dressed in 3 piece suit, a trilby hat pulled low over his eyes. His purposeful stride was, well - purposeful. The rich brown attaché case swung back and forth as he neared the entrance.

The overall architecture of the place was an oddSods kinda structure. Way back - way back about twenty years ago it had been the only service station within thirty miles of here.

Jed, who now owned the place and operated it with his wife Gracie and their teenage twins, had put a fair degree of effort but not a lot of money into what was the only restaurant diner in the area.

Inventiveness, ingenuity and an ability to re-purpose old barn wood, sections of window glass and old doors had been somewhat woven into the interior envelope.

It was a little wonky but a lot happy crazy in the general look and feel.

In an attempt to counteract the fierce winter winds that blasted across the adjacent open fields Jed had constructed smallish entry porch. It was just big enough such that when a group of four or five descended upon the place, they could all crowd into the unheated porch area allowing the first door to close behind them before they opened the actual interior door. Everyone in the town agreed that Jed had put some good thinking into providing this little welcoming handshake to his customers. Mabes always thought of it as an airlock between the vast emptiness of the surrounding area and the comfort of this old place.

As the man drew nearer Mabes perked up a little for certainly this guy was very much out of character and context in this remote little part of Kansas.

'I mean', she muttered to herself. Only old Doc the local funeral home director even owned a three piece suit, let alone wore one.

She heard the first door open, but as the inside door had no window, she knew only that he was suddenly in that buffer zone.

She waited expectantly for the inner door to open. She now, very much wanted to verify that her vision and/or her brain, had not undergone a massive fail in seeing what she believed she had seen.

But the moments drew outwards. The inside door did not open.

She sat more erect, shaking her head a bit.

'Did you see that guy?' She asked aloud.

'What guy? There ain't no guy.' Josie replied, snapping his newspaper.

'Jed - Jed. What the fuck man? Guy just came into the porch, hasn't left. He's still out there. Whaddaya think he's up to?'

Jed paused in his scraping of the big flat grill plate, turned towards her, and then looked towards the door.

'Dunno - maybe he's talkin' on his phone for a minute. What's the big deal?'

'Well - it's just weird', she replied. 'A businessman type guy in a three piece suit - where the hell you think he came from. Weird.'

Josie, peering up over his paper, eyed her suspiciously.

'C'mon Mabes. Old Hubie been beatin' on ya again last night? Plying you with that homemade moonshine shit? That's why yer in here looking' hungover and bent sideways?'

'Fuck you Josie - leave old Hubie outta this. None yer business anyways. I'm gonna go check this shit out.'

She placed her hands on the counter to push herself back off the stool.

The door suddenly opened and standing there was a total surprise to her mussed up brain.

A man in one of those old, wrinkled, weather-worn Australian greatcoats, a backpack hanging from his left hand. On his head was a way outta place Montréal Expos baseball cap.

She sat down, mouth agape. She turned towards Jed, wanting to say something but there was no words.

Josie looked over to the door his eyes creased as he squinted at what he was seeing.

Nobody spoke for a moment as the stranger surveyed the room.

'G'day mates', he said finally in a clear Australian accent. 'How y'all doin' this fine winter's morn?'

"Ahhhhh . . . . ahhhh', Mabes started. And as she attempted to say something - anything at all, she was also leaning to her left, trying to see behind the stranger.

The stranger's smile widened almost impossibly big, showing a mouthful of what seemed to be larger than normal, very white teeth.

'K', he said. 'Guess cat's got yer tongue. No worries. But I'm sure looking for some nice hot breakfast.'

Looking towards Jed he swung his backpack up in a general arc and asked, 'Anywheres you want me to set?'

Jed also was mouth agape as this completely out of the norm apparition berated at him.

' Uhhh - no - seat yourself. Anywheres you like.'

The stranger swept the room with his gaze, stopped at Mabes, and said, 'Ma'am - mind if I set myself down besides you there?'

Mabes was looking like a fresh caught bass on the bottom of a rowboat, gasping for breath.

'Uh - no. It's fine - all good. Whatever you'd like.'

As he moved to the end of the u-shaped counter Mabes pushed herself back upright, standing in the aisle space.

'Gotta git to the Ladies', she mumbled.

She moved down the aisle space and passed him close by.

Graciously the stranger drew himself inwards allowing her space to move past him.

Rounding the end of the counter she made a bee-line past the doorway towards the open kitchen area, and then pushed open the door marked 'Ladies/Gents'.

The stranger moved down towards where Mabes had been sitting and in doing so passed Josie. He stopped, stuck out his hand and loudly proclaimed, 'Hey there. Name's Rufus. Nice to meetya.'

Josie stammered, 'Ahh - sure, yeah. Nice to meetya too', as he allowed his hand to be swallowed up in huge grip of this stranger.

'So my man', Jed started. 'Set yourself there - just give yerself some space between you and Mabes. She hates to feel crowded. Menu's right there. Give it a look - lemme know what you'd like.'

Rufus dropped his backpack with a heavy 'clump'.

Josie would have sworn later he heard metal striking against the old flooring when it landed.

Rufus straddled the old red vinyl chrome-banded stool and got himself comfortable.

'Let's just see what we got here', he said, mostly to himself.

He gripped the old time-worn plastic laminated menus sheet and started to read it.

Josie went back to his newspaper with a drawn-out sigh.

Rufus, eyes narrowing, glanced over towards him just as the washroom door opened and Mabes walked out.

She paused mid-step as she noticed the scene in front of her, kinda frozen in time.

But suddenly she turned to her left saying over her shoulder, 'Hey Jed … .gotta git sumpin' outta the truck.'

Jed grunted, Rufus smiled broadly at her.

She huddled into herself as she exited out into the biting morning prairie winds, her neck scrunched down into herself. As she got to the gravel edge of the parking area, she looked for her truck and both Josie's old car and Jed's station wagon.

And of course, the stranger's vehicle.

But there were only three there.

She stopped, cold, at the front of her truck.

Beyond puzzled, she slowly revolved in a full circle, thinking she might see something that quite simply, was simply, not there.

Completely puzzled now, she moved, with no urgency, slowly, to the driver's door, opened it, pulled herself up onto the seat, and – just sat there.

'This is making no sense!, she thought.

'Where did he come from?', she questioned. 'How did he get here?'

She sat for a spell, pondering. It was beginning to feel like a dream sequence.

'Might be he had had hitch-hiked and someone dropped him off! Yes!', she concluded, 'Gotta be how it happened.'

Reaching that conclusion, the norms of an unsophisticated mind clicked back into place, and she turned, opened the cab door and dropped to the ground.

A Kiss May Be

We weren't supposed to be there.

And so, what then took place was, one could say, simply serendipity.

But, being there, huddled under the tree branches, trying to shield ourselves from the tumultuous flash thunderstorm - well, it became, rather unintentionally comical.

Worse was the fact that we didn't know one another. At all.

As I glanced sideways, trying not to appear as if I was looking, I was quite flushed by her appearance. The dark, springy curly hair that peeked out from beneath the oh-so-stylish hat - a beige linen I think, with a crimson band about it that was also trimmed in a deep lush purple pinstripe. Reminded me of Ingrid Bergman in Casablanca. And she had that very aloof, sophisticated demeanor about her. Coupled with the butterscotch flavored belted raincoat, with a high voluptuous collar, flaring epaulets with cream-coloured ivory buttons....it was - well it, and she, was a picture.

But awkward it was. Neither had an umbrella. As I continued to steal glances it was quite apparent that she could, if she chose to, use the rich brown leather shoulder bag as a sortof makeshift roof, by holding it above her head. But in a flash it seemed clear that she'd rather risk the chapeau getting soaked rather than possibly defacing that beautiful bag.

Suddenly, things changed - at the same time as the earth shifted. Well quite possibly she didn't sense the shift - it was probably just me. For I was, falling in - well, like....but real serious like, you know. Her? Not so much. Of that I'm quite sure.

But the real change was the explosive crack of thunder - so loud, so close that she instinctively jumped towards me. I, of course, was startled out of a dream state. After all, I had begun to not care a whit about getting wet - not as long as this storm could continue on. 'Cause whilst it lasted, well - where was she gonna go?

But, taken aback as I was I put out one arm to break her fall against me. As she stumbled, she looked up at me with black black eyes, frightened like a fawn, skittish like a kitten.

She tried to smile but was collected proper by her embarassment. I felt it, actually.

Caused my cheeks to flame, I'm sure,

'Pardon', I mumbled dumbly. 'So sorry...' with my arm still about her shoulder. And the fabric of the trenchcoat felt so - well, luxurious. Like when you fall into a bed with freshly pressed high thread count sheets.

She righted herself, but couldn't really move away from me for the rain that was heavy before was now a torrent....and the only little circle that it was not intruding on was the circle of new warmth created by our unintentional - togetherness.

And so, we did, what we had to do. She looked off to her right, I looked off to my left, as we stood there, raindrops splattering and exploding up off the pavement.

And then, 'Oh! Look! Look there, quick!' she exclaimed pointing directly in front, across the road.

Lightning had pierced the night sky directly in front of us.

And just as it was fading, we saw - both of us, at the same time, the grim outline of an old Packard, driver's window down, and the secondary lightning flash of a camera bulb pointed directly at us.

eight items or less

Was the only one in line, was idly watching but not seeing anything. I had placed the contents of my cart on the belt. Heard a voice - took a second to realize she was talking to me.

'Real nice steaks you got there..... now that's a dinner party I'd like to go to...'

I looked over at the cashier.
Smiled

She smiled back - a lovely smile. Except it showed the gaps where two of her upper teeth were missing.

But it was real warm. And a twinkling eye. Or, as she turned to look at me full-face, I instantly wondered if the twinkly eye might be due to the fact that it was what you call, a lazy eye.

But she smiled again....

And of course I said, 'Well I figured that....clearly you recognize quality when you see it.'

She grinned, real warm at me.

'Yep...I do. And I ain't no cheap date!'

'Could see that immediately', I replied.

'Watcha makin' anyways?'

'Music, Honey', I said with a smile....

'So far, it's sounding like a nice melody'

She smiled, a lazy, warm glow.....I melted a little.

'Sally', her name tag read.

'So, Sally - time to get cooking......'

'Yep', she said, breaking the moment.

Turning back to busy herself at the register, she looked back at me - that smile again, and winked.

'I'll bring the desert', she grinned.

'Honey - you are a desert.... a real treat.'

Awkward moment there.

'So - for sure - I'll be out front waiting - at what time?', I asked.

'Six o'clock - get off at six', she replied.

'Six 'tis', as I picked up my bags, our fingers touched as she handed the receipt to me.

'See ya then'

'Yeah - see you then', she said.

Flight Delayed

It was supposed to have been easy – real easy.

Same as it's been about a dozen times previously…..on a flight out of Montreal to

Ft. Lauderdale – hang around a bit, then connect on a flight to Freeport, Grand Bahama.

Why Freeport? Well, I have these great friends/clients – we go back about 30 years….. Designed their beach house – 30 miles outside of Freeport. It really is, special. No – it's a whole lot special……

And it is – usually easy. Little puddle jumper aircraft – 30 minutes from lift-off to touchdown. Simple.

Except this time it wasn't. This time was different……the first part though was easy. Arrived FLL at about 1:00 PM on Sunday – texted my buddy Ryan who picked me up. We went for a fabulous lunch at My Big Fat Greek restaurant.

Dropped me back at the airport at 4:00 PM for my 7:00 o' clock flight. All easy.

Boarded on time – was one of those little twin prop jobs, one seat on each side of the aisle…..and we taxied out of the gate at about the right time. This aircraft had two sliding doors between the flight deck and the passenger area, that closed in the middle – but the latch wasn't working, so, as we would take a turn on the runway, a door would slide back….and as there was no flight attendant, the co-pilot had to reach behind him and try to yank the door closed again. How's that for cockpit security?

As I was in the second row, whenever the door slid open I had a direct view into the cockpit. To me, just a confusing jumble of dials and toggle switches.

So – we idled at the end of the runway awaiting tower instructions to turn into the take-off lane.

The thrumming of the engines, combined with the heat, the big lunch, was making me very sleepy. I would doze off – jerk awake, only to find that maybe a minute had passed.

I suppose the next time I dozed off, a greater time had passed, because next thing I know, we're airborne at cruising altitude. As I looked at my watch 7:25 Figured we were 75% to our destination. It was about– not quite dark, but getting there……

As I rested my head against the window, still half asleep I could see the co-pilot gesticulating, pointing to a couple of gauges and one of the switchbanks overhead.

Of course, with the drone of the engines I couldn't hear anything. And, I was really only halfways aware of it all.

Dozed again - was brought wide awake by a loud crack just near my head….against the side of the fuselage. I jumped, alert – my glance caught a sight of the co-pilot wrestling the yoke to port…..I looked at the window. The outside was covered in a bloody smear.

'What the hell is going on?', I remember yelling.

Plane lurched to port – to the left, the nose swung down at a steep angle. I grabbed the side of the armrest. The woman across the aisle from me was shrieking. I could hear shouting back and forth from the cockpit.

Looked again quickly at the bloody mess smeared across my window, and almost threw up. An eyeball was dead center, in a pile of slick blood and tissue, the strings of muscle or whatever, streaming back along the glass.

My brain knew it was an eyeball……my brain realized that it probably wasn't human.

But was, sure ugly and messy. A couple of whitish feathers slid across the glass and I realised that we must have hit a bird of some kind. The propeller, just beyond, was stuttering….would return to smooth rotation, then would kindof stop/stall.

The nose of the aircraft was following a corkscrew, downwards to the left. The angle felt impossible! Everyone behind and around me was shouting. A baby was screaming somewhere. The doors to the cockpit were banging closed and sliding open.

Everyone was freaked.

A voice came over the intercom.

'Please try to remain calm. We've had a mid-air incident – involved some birds. They hit the propellers of the port engine. We're doing our best to correct the situation. Keep your seatbelts on, and hold tight. We may have to ditch. If we do we are only about a mile offshore, and we should be fine.'

'Shit!', my brain said. You always half-listen to all those pre-flight instructions – the ones about flotation devices, and tubes, and blowing and sucking – all that crap. And you never really hear it.

We all kindof calmed down a little…….the pilot corrected the crazy corkscrew turn of the plane, and we started to level off again. But it was fairly dark now. Could not see how close or far away from the water we were.

The plane started to turn right – to starboard. Then I could see quite clearly – the port engine stopped. And smoke started to drift out of the housing.

As the doors slid back and forth it was apparent, that although the flight crew wasn't panicked, there was a lot of desperate wrestling with the controls going on.

The plane started again to level off, but seemed to be dropping rapidly.

Then with a bang as we hit!

The seatbelt prevented me from whacking my head against the overhead.

My breath exploded out of my body. Someone – or two or three – or everyone, started to scream, to cry, to swear. I'm sure I was doing my share.

The plane bounced – seemed to be airborne once again, then the nose tilted down, sickeningly, like in a roller coaster drop, and it must have dug into a wave because then everything went crazy – really crazy.

The body slewed to the right....I felt, weirdly as if we were a stone, skipping across the water. Just like when I was a little kid and we'd throw flat stones against the waves of the lake and see whose could take the most number of skips.

It was dizzying, sickening because everything was now a blur as we spun wildly.

Then we hit something – had no idea what it was. Someone later said they thought it might have been an abandoned pier pipe sticking out of the water.

We hit it on the right side, which was lucky for me as I was on the opposite side.

Not so lucky, as it turns out, for the poor woman sitting across the aisle from me.

The plane bounced back....there was a terrible crumpling sound. The engines stopped. There was, for a second – maybe only three or four, silence.

Then I was aware of the pilot, or the co-pilot, stumbling out of the cockpit, blood streaming down his face. A large gash was bleeding badly. He struggled to hold himself upright, and as he did so, he yelled out, 'Everyone – get out of your seatbelts – grab the seat cushions – move forward to exit here at the front. Try to be calm about this – it seems worse than it is. Help is on the way.'

There was panicked movement all about me. I thought about my laptop and camera in the overhead bin. Did I dare to try to grab it? Didn't matter – I couldn't get out of my seat. The pilot was blocking the aisle trying to un-fasten the seat belt of the lady across from me, who was, at the very least, unconscious.

We always hear, on TV, or in movies, 'Don't panic!' Have you ever panicked? And, what is panic? Is it the burst of sweat over your heart and on your forehead as you realize, 'This is serious…..I gotta get outta here!' Whatever it is, I had it…….the co-pilot had come to help the pilot……they struggled to un-latch the seat belt.

Meanwhile the passengers had nowhere to go…..they were backed up in the narrow aisleway, pushing and shoving. I couldn't move. I was completely blocked in.

Mostly all you heard was the slap of the waves against the fuselage between the yells, screams and curses of all onboard.

Finally, with a resounding click, they un-did the belt. One lifted her out of the seat – the other grabbed her under her arms and they struggled to move towards the doorway. Water was now lapping about our feet, as the plane was settling.

As soon as they managed to get her body by my seat I attempted to stand up but was hit by someone – someone very big, and dazedly I fell back against the fuselage.

My head was spinning, I tasted blood in my mouth. I was vaguely aware of pushing and shoving in the aisleway as the dozen or so passengers fought and struggled towards the entrance. Dimly I thought everyone had passed, and I tried to pull myself upright, but as soon as I got almost to a standing position, everything changed. The plane lurched, as a wing was swamped by a wave, and I fell back hitting my head. It was the last thing I remembered as everything got fuzzy black.

As I slipped into unconsciousness, I do remember, vaguely hearing another scream of panic….I'm not sure but It sounded like, 'OhMiGod! What was that? Is that a shark? Help!!!'

. . . .

The coolness of a soft breeze was washing over me. A sensation of cool, crisp sheets against my skin was a comforting feeling as soft light began to nudge me into consciousness. It might have been that I was wrapped in a cassock, ready to meet the Maker……what it was was clean white cotton fitted against my body, snugly.

My eyelids fluttered….my breath caught. I must have made a sound for suddenly both my hands were grasped by others. One, soft and comforting – the other rough and strong.

'Michael. Michael. Can you hear? Hello?'

It was like a long distance telephone call, fading in/out. My head was woozy, mouth was dry, eyes gritty as I tried to open and focus.

'Hey Buddy!', a deeper voice resonated. 'You in there? You okay?'

'Nurse is coming……try to relax – you're safe…you're okay.'

After a moment or two of washing dizziness, another voice chimed in.

'Mr. Moore – you're okay. You're in Freeport Clinic, and in good hands. Dr. Miller will be in shortly to see you. Do you want water? Here – take a sip – not too much now…..'

And gentle hands raised my head so I could manipulate the straw in my mouth. Nothing ever tasted so good……cool, clear water washing over my tongue, through my mouth, back to the deep back of my throat.

I think I drifted off once again, for next thing I remember was actually waking up – like after a long night's sleep. But to darkness and stillness. My eyes popped open – and scanned the ceiling. A gentle light framed the space beyond the bed. I didn't move for many moments as I recalled those last minutes of panic in the aircraft.

'I'm alive....I'm alive, at least', I said to myself. 'I guess the rest can only be okay.'

I turned my head to the left, and the movement must have woken her, because next I heard was, 'Michael....it's Del. You're back – you're okay. Do you want more water? I need to call the nurse. Just don't move – everything is going to be fine. I'll be right back'

Well, some days have passed – not many, but it's remarkable how one can recover from such horrendous events so quickly.

As various people spoke with me, clued me in, the story became clearer. Yes – the plane crashed – a freak accident. Happens, so I'm told. And I know that to be true.

Yes – there was pain and suffering – but no loss of life. The lady across the aisle from me actually brought me tea and cookies a day or so later. She's okay – at least physically. The flight crew have been celebrated for their coolness and bravery......even my laptop and camera were recovered as the plane didn't actually sink.

Seems the collision with the birds caused a mechanical mal-function in engine one.....but the pilot and co-pilot were remarkable in the way they handled the forced landing – and in the way they shepherded the passengers to safety.

I actually asked about the sharks – and yes – there were sharks in the waters thereabouts. But, apparently they are predominantly nurse sharks – a fairly benign type of shark. But, I was also told, there is always a couple of hammerhead sightings in that area every summer.

So – I'm recovering now. I will spend the rest of the week at Bill & Del's – in the villa adjacent to their beachhouse. It is lovely and tranquil – with a 40 foot long screened porch overlooking the Caribbean. And I may even end up finishing the job – the project – which they brought me here for in the first place.

I suppose, quite simply, the lesson learned is, don't ever take things for granted. Life can change in the blink of an eye.

ABOUT DONE

'So - that about does it.'

I looked up at him. Tall, rangy - sweat-soaked. Backwards baseball cap with a ring of sweat along the band.

Yeah, was hot. Was fucking hot. Humid too.

And I know it was a long - a very long day.

'Wanna beer?', I asked. My tone telling him, 'better not, you ain't really seen, cranky.'

He looked at me, hands on his hips.

Read me. Correctly. I felt it.

'Nah!', he managed.

I could see, out of the corner of my eye, that Melissa sure as hell wanted a beer.

'Maybe just one', she said.

Just the way I was feeling.

Apartment was now all packed up, cleaned out - 'cept for the chair I was sitting on, a cot bed in the alcove, and barstool at the counter. Plus a whole bunch of what you used to call, *knick knax*........

As movers, the two of them were well paired. Efficient, quiet, focused. Good.

The silence sat heavy around the space now. The gloom was only slightly dispelled. The not-quite-there light that came from the single low wattage bulb that hung over the bar countergave it a good shot. Spent, though, pretty much - as was I.

I sighed and said, 'Okay. What's the damage here now? How much?'

Spud - that's what I'd taken to calling him in my mind, withdrew a little spiral bound notebook from his top left pocket. Had to unsnap the pearl button first. 'Course, wasn't really pearl. One of them fake synthetic things they put on cowboy shirts.

He paused, looked at me. Meanwhile I had waved Melissa, with a half-hearted motion, over to the old fridge. She got it. And, she got it

'1200 dollars', he said. 'Wanna breakdown? It's all here.'

I closed my eyes for a bit, squinged.

Was gonna hurt. I knew it.

After a deep sigh, I pulled myself up saying, as I did, 'No problem Bub. You earned it.'

And I proceeded to count out twelve hundred dollar bills. Hesitated for a moment, added another one to it.

I looked closely at him as I held it out.

'You both earned it - hope it helps a tad.'

Reaching for it he smiled.

'Pleasure doin' business with you Man.'

We both regarded one another, quietly.

The mood in the apartment was gritty and it was decidedly blue. It felt like wood smoke was crawling up under my t-shirt.

I squinted. I squinted 'cause I was all of a sudden facing and forcing down, the sudden flush of tears.

Had to get him outta there. Her too.

Needed aloneness....

'No problem. If I had any faith that there might be a 'next time', well, I'd say somethin' dumb probably'

As she passed me she raised the beer bottle in her right hand, in like, a salute.

Said nothing.

They moved to the door, opened it and started to walk out onto the little landing at the top of the stairs.

At the last possible moment, she turned back, looked at me and smiled.

I said, like an idiot, 'Seeya guys - was a pleasure working with you.'

And then more directly, at her, 'And a pleasure watching you work'.

She winked at me and then, they were gone.

'Doofus, moi!'

Silence was now painting the space.

I stood there and sighed.

I stood there and suddenly, thought of you, again.

Not that I wasn't, sadly, always thinking about you. But the intense working and pushing and shlepping over the last few hours had kept you in your place.

Still in my heart, but tucked up and away from more conscious dwelling.

Now, of course, there was no protection of a distraction of stuff needing to be done.

It was over.

It was all over, and I, was done.

I paused, leaning up against the wall, only half seeing the space around me.

My head drooped to see only the old fussy stained floorboards.

And my breath caught in my chest and then my breath caught in my throat.

It was suffocating, this facing real reality.

It was fucking painful, with nowhere to turn to, nowhere to turn to where you weren't somehow there - with that smile, with the crinkle of your tinkling laugh.

The pain, like a popcorn ball, rose in my chest.

I knew I had to deal with some things. Knew I had to order some of the disorder still left here. about. Knew I had to find a way to make it through the night to arrive at a cold morning when I would make my last exit from this space, close the door, slip the key under it, never to return.

A few - very few things left to do. The box - it was all that was left aside from my bumpy-bump travel bag.

Walking across the echo I lifted the box up onto the counter.

Stopped, stared at it. Felt the dull edge of the hanging light bulb as it sawed its way into the gloom.

Opening the top flap I started to pull things out. And I looked at each one as I did. And with the very first one I questioned my fucking sanity for ever thinking this was a good idea. But, like biting down on a sore tooth, I pushed, myself.

The first thing was a lovely photograph of a lovely you, gazing at the camera, your head held between both hands, with a smile that instantly shredded my heart. I put it aside. I paused and then fished out the next thing. A journal book you had given me.

I remembered vividly when. It was on the occasion of our first anniversary. With a glass of red wine in one hand you reached down into your bag on the floor and with a smile, laid the package on the table, saying,

'I searched far and wide to find this - for you. It, suits you and I hope you like it.'

The white tissue paper had a simple burgundy ribbon about it which, while blowing you a kiss, I unwrapped, exclaiming as the supple butterscotch leather of the cover was revealed.

'It's gorgeous', I exclaimed, quickly removing the balance of the tissue. 'Really gorgeous! Thank you - so very much. I will use it for my special writing - for the poems I write about you, for you.'

And you smiled, deeply, reaching across the table to grasp my hand, inter-twining your fingers into mine.

Cocking your head to one side you replied, 'And I will always treasure those poems, J,. Truly I will'

'I love it when you call me 'J', I replied.

And with that I reached inside my blazer, and withdrew a slim package.

I held it out to you, saying as I did, 'Did you think I forgot? Never', I said.

You looked stern. Or you tried to look stern.

'I told you - I'm not good with getting gifts. Wish you hadn't but makes me happy that you did. Thank you.'

And with that you peeled off the wrapping, opened the little box to reveal, sitting on a satin bed, a Mont Blanc pen. But a white Mont Blanc.

You gasped

'How gorgeous', you said and I smiled for again you warmed my heart so completely.

You withdrew it, feeling it in your hand.

'It has a beautiful feel - sensuous - like you', she said smiling at me.

I grinned at her.

If you look closely on the clip, I had it engraved', I said

You looked and exclaimed, 'It's to me! I think it's to me. Says 'Princess'- is that right?', you asked raising an eyebrow.

'It is.', I replied. 'Because you are, a princess'

And all these memories flooded back across my nerve endings, so raw, so painfully.

I stood there gripping the counter edge trying to stop myself from falling over.

And I knew that journal and that photograph would be two of the things I would carry with me throughout my life.

Turning, I reached behind me - yanked the refrigerator door open and reached inside to grab another beer.

I had no desire to continue. The flashbacks were like a coarse steel brush scraping across a sunburned body.

But although I wanted just to take the box and toss the rest of its contents into a dumpster I couldn't do that.

So, after a few moments, I resolutely carried on.

Blindly fumbling within I pulled out another framed photograph. Looking at it I felt the tension grip along my chest. I forced myself to look at it, because although it showed the three of us, which is what rankled and irritated me, you, your smile, was such a brilliant sun flare that I knew I'd have hard time disposing of it. I also knew, instinctively, that I should keep it, scan it and when I had the time, do some digital Photoshop magic - and cut out, excise, that undeserving and unwelcome other guy, from the photograph.

Oddly, after that, the rest was easier. Was a lot more comfortable to separate the contents into a pile 'A' and a pile 'B'.

At the end, pile 'A' was comprised of 6 things. All things that brought your life back into my life.

I took everything from pile 'B' and put it back into the box. Opening a side pouch of my carry bag I slipped my treasures inside, closed it up, and sat heavily, on the barstool, literally drained and draped over the counter.

Was time.

Now, was time. Sleep, if possible. Wake at the appropriate time. Leave, walk down the stairs for the last time, to wait for the pre-arranged Uber that would take me to the Greyhound bus terminal.

And as I passed through the doorway - what had been once, our doorway, I knew I'd carry with me my last vision of you -standing there door opened, bags at your feet, anger flushing your countenance, intolerance gripping your face, as you said to me, 'We're done - you know that. I'm going back to my home in Paris. I do not, expect, nor do I want, to hear from you - ever again.'

And with that, you left.

And with that, I remained - trying desperately to understand.

Mulberry Bushes and Christmastime

'Must be that', one bobby said to the other as they waited under the elegant awning.

'Aye – that's what I bin hearing at the station house Lad – what with this COVID stuff the department is stretched to breaking.'

'Would explain why we've been told to come investigate what is probably a petty theft or something – must be that his Lordship here is well connected.'

'Well – instructions are to show up, be nice – do a polite investigation and then wait for a detective to come and review with us......sure seems like a waste of resources to me....'

'Ahh – here we go', he said as the glossy black door swung open on it's bright, brass hinges.

'Kin I help you officers?' the maid asked. 'Is this about the break-in?'

'Tis', the older bobby replied. 'May we come in and survey the situation?'

She stepped back swinging the door wide open to reveal a gleaming, polished black and white checkerboard marble floor.

They entered, removing their helmets as they did so.

'Need we remove boots and so on?', they asked her.

'No – not necessary – please come in – it's just this way, down the hall a bit.'

They followed her along the hallway painted in a deep lacquer Chinese red. With all the stair railings and trim in shiny black it was a striking space.

She paused at a double door entry, rapped on the door and getting no response opened it ushering them into the room.

Beside the Georgian fireplace, in the corner near the bay window, was a towering Christmas tree in a semi completed state of trimming.

'Pardon the bit of a mess – as you can see we're in the last stages of prepping for Christmas.'

Both officers were somewhat mesmerized by the grandeur of the space, the period furnishings now pushed back against the walls, the beautiful artwork that graced the room.

The maid led them to the centre of the room to a fairly large round mahogany table – the kind with the splayed base and brass-tipped feet.

'See everything on the table here? These are various presents we were in the process of wrapping etcetera when we left this task to deal with some other issues in one of the local shops. So when we left the house this is almost exactly the state things were in in this room.'

'I see', the senior bobby said. 'And so what is the problem? We were asked to investigate a break-in here. Is there evidence of that which we might examine?'

'Yes – over here at the window. See how the latch is snapped off? We believe that whilst we were out the thief forced the window and entered there.', she said pointing to some scrapes and scratches on the overly wide sill.

The officers bent to look closer. The younger one removed a smallish camera from his tunic and snapped some photographs.

They turned to her and asked, 'So – can you tell us what was stolen? Silverware? China – artwork?'

'Well, see – that's the problem – we can't pin down anything that was taken. It's very curious is it not?'

'Indeed – 'tis. And for how long were you absent from the premises?'

'All told about 45 minutes. Perhaps we frightened him off when we came in the front door. We assume so because the window was still open when we came in here and it was rather cold then.'

'Okay – can you spend a little time with us and we'll do a quick inventory in the room here first? Our superior is expected to pop along soon – just to check in as a courtesy call to assure his Lordship that we are doing all we can.'

'Yes – of course. Shall we start with the table here?'

The two bobbies looked at one another thinking, probably, something like 'But these are just a collection of Christmas presents.'

However, politely they replied, 'Yes – of course. Might we make a list of all that's on the table and you can provide details, comments?'

They spent ten minutes or so picking up objects, the younger officer noting a description in his notebook, the older bobby carefully examining each as he passed it along.

After a bit there was one item left to be examined and record. It was a very colourful, odd looking thing with a bright yellow handle on one side.

Just then the doorbell chimed and the maid, excusing herself, went to answer.

A rustle of fabric caused them to turn to the door where they saw their superior officer entering the room.

The broad bustle of her skirt, a black taffeta, swished as she passed a chair and made her way to the table where they stood.

She was well known to the officers as she was to the entire force as she was, to say the least, rather extravagant in both manner and dress. Her hat, black also, sat precariously on her head, its brim flowing gracefully down over her forehead, a delicate veil pinned to one side of the brim.

With a flourish she raised her silver-tipped cane to tap gently on the mahogany table.

'And what is all this about?, she asked imperiously. 'Have we established a list of what's been stolen?'

'Not quite yet Guv'nor', the older bobby answered. 'But we're just now recording the last item that was here', he said pointing to the table.

'I see', she said.' And what is that you are holding?'

He had, it appeared, forgotten it was still in his hand.

'Oh this? Well we're not exactly sure……this odd little handle….'and as he said it, he gave it a twist. The top popped open and a bright red spring was released.

They all looked in surprise as the spring, now freed, quivered back and forth.

Recovering their composure, the maid, bent more closely turned her head and said,

'Mum – it would appear that what is actually missing here is simply the Jack from this

Jack-in-the-Box.'

'Quite!', stated the detective. 'Quite indeed.' Looking at the two bobbies, then at the maid, she gave them a firm nod and said, as she turned to sweep out of the room, 'Carry on then – I'll expect a full report stat.'

Hello There

'Hello'

Heard the soft greeting out of my right ear – voice coming from behind me, but faintly.

Automatic presumption was, someone greeting someone – else.

'Hello?', this time a little louder with a clear question mark attached to it.

Still, in my reverie simply did not occur that it was any different than my initial presumption. Carried on, lost in some sad and unhappy thoughts. Watched limply as the cotton clouds drifted and shape-shifted across the sky.

Was an usual day in Montreal – still April, early in April. And there was warmth – warmth from a warming sun. Warming the air about, but also, gently warming the air in my soul.

And it was so welcome – felt a touch like when warmed up peanut butter oozes welcomingly over the lip of the bowl.

Lost in the weightlessness of a moment – a rare and easy moment.

'Hello!'

This time I could actually see the exclamation mark, or point! Like a dagger, sharp, insistent.

I turned – felt I had no choice but to respond somehow, resentment burbling within a shell of hostility that I was being deprived – distracted from such a special and rarely visited place.

But, she was beautiful! Prickliness of pissed-offed-ness, slid away.

She was standing there, cloaked, in a cloak. Black, deep black – resonating of darkest nights but fringed with a border of rich reds, greens and golds – of a pattern borrowed from the softest of kilims.

She leaned into her cane, which a quick glance showed it to be an ebony stick topped with an ornately carved silver horse's head. Gripped by patent leather gloves, lacquered against the form of her hands – walking up her forearms to just below her elbows.

But the hat, the hat was a masterpiece! It was an announcement – a trumpet blast to anyone who may not have responded to the resonance of all the other parts and pieces of this painting.

My breath caught – due in part, probably to the total unexpectedness of this vision, here, in this out-of-the-way raggedy park. If park is an accurate term for the space. More of a neglected strip of a greenspace necklace that bordered this lagoon of the St. Lawrence River.

'I'm sorry', I said. Said it with genuine feeling and sincerity. Her pouty lips curled up in the schizophrenic rictus between a smile and a smirk.

Hard to say, with any accuracy, which it was.

But – I'd take it I decided.

'I'm sorry – wasn't aware you were addressing me. Can I – can I, uh - - be of any assistance? Are you okay?', as I gestured to her cane. 'Would you care to sit – here?'

Her porcelain countenance slowly rotated to look out over the lagoon. I looked about me as she seemed to become pre-occupied with the frame of her vision.

We were, alone, here, now. Other park visitors had left – I was aware of a general dissolution of the construct of the sky. The clouds, which had so recently embraced me here, had dissolved into a grey muddy mass. The air became currents as a wind, from origins of the north, began a crafty bite into my cheek.

Turning back she also turned her face to me at the same time.

'Yes', she said, simply.

I waited. She waited, no movement, but her gaze trapped mine in a crystalline cloak of capture.

'Yes', again, she said softly.' I expect I'd like to sit here, if you feel it not to be an intrusion.'

She moved – lifted her cane, lifted one leg, leather clad in painted on calf skin, towards the bench.

I, magnaminously, as if I was a regent, waved grandly to the space to my right.

'Please – please do.'

And she did. With a fluidity that belied any dependence on the supporting cane.

Turning to me, she crossed one leg over the other. Placed her left arm on the bench back, and cupped her delicate chin in her left hand, gazing, intently at me.

The obsidian cast of her eyes, probing and penetrating, laser-like, bore into me.

'So tell me', she whispered huskily, 'Have you been waiting long?'

All The Best Laid Plans

'Wait – you'll see. This is gonna be great. Better than great. That's if you agree to help out here.'

'I'm not interested, in the least, in your most wonderfully great and latest scheme.', she replied, arching her eyebrow.

'And why do you always do this to me? Always. You take off – are gone for days, sometimes a text – sometimes a voice message – and then....', she was starting to sputter as the anger took hold. 'And then', as she whipped the thermos cup away from her body, the hot chocolate hitting the freshly fallen snow and creating little streams, dots and dashes on the fine crystal surfaces. 'And then, you show up on my doorstep, as if – as if...'

He held up his hand to stop the stream he knew would follow.

'It's the smile', the thought flitted across the headache fault lines that were forming.

'It's that fucking smile and the goofy grin, that does it to me.'

'You never give me a chance to explain. You're just – you're just too selfish.' he asserted.

'Me!', she screamed. 'Me? Me selfish? I give you everything you ask for – I give you money, I give you support – I give you....', as she caught her breath, her chest now heaving, 'I give you – freedom.'

He sat there, on the log at the side of the trail, legs spread, boots splayed.

'Yes – I do – I give you the one thing you never actually ask for – freedom. And this is how you repay me.'

Her head hanging, she stared down at the snow, lost in her thoughts.

He knew well enough to shut up. He knew well enough to let her have it run its course.

He knew well enough to know, he would, once again, win her over, win her back.

After a few moments – maybe minutes, she raised her head, turned her face to him.

The golden silky frame of hair that graced the beauty of her face, once again, caught in his chest. For a moment – for a minute.

With a look as contrite as he could muster, he said to her softly, 'You're right – as you are always right. I am, all that – all those things. But I am that way because I feel an uncontrollable desperation to succeed. To make these ideas, these projects work – to work for me, and to work for you,' And with the greatest sincerity he could bring to his face, 'For us.'

And she melted, once again.

With a sniffle and a swipe of her mitten across her nose, she finally looked again at him.

'You do know there is one constant in all these grand ideas, don't you? One constant flaw that will forever prevent you from bringing the realization of any of these ideas to me, to us?'

Sheepishly, he looked up and over at her.

'And what – what might that be?' he asked somewhat belligerently.

She sighed, took a deep breath and looked him straight in the eye.

'You are ceaseless in your efforts, if not permanently misguided. You may, or may not, ever learn that lesson.'

'Go on', he said

'It's simple – in your cockiness and your arrogance you have never learned this one simple lesson………Man plans, and God laughs.'

Light in the Dark

There was, as there is with all things, a beginning. But, she couldn't exactly remember where, or when that was now; nor how far she, and the group had navigated from that point of origin. Someone had led the way. Until they could no longer, and it had been a responsibility that only she could effectively manage. Given the developing apparent seriousness of the situation, as unclear as it still was – it was certainly no justification for being so woefully ignorant. But as is often the case if one is unaware of a tsunami's approach, one tends to allow ones' self to drift. Until it's too late to take the appropriate cautionary protective measures.

That they had reached a certain waypoint now, dawned slowly on them –on all of them.
The awareness that the mounting evidence as provided to them was like a glistening stone breaking through the crystalline ice of last night's storm – as the reality and the attendant fears revealed themselves.

To most of the others –but not to him, she was quite sure – the realization was slow in arriving. And of course, not having the benefit of knowledge or the recognition of any kind of a sign, the others had kinda meandered along, following this lead. In a slightly drunken force of movement, surely as unpredictable as flotsam, their course seemed to be not so defined by a timetable as it was by rather a pulsating magnetic pull. She attempted to provide a skeleton of possible explanation – one that she herself was grasping to form in long tapering fingers – a plausible frame of understanding that the others might see, that they might clutch in a somnolent desire to make some sense from the fragments of the facts available.

But as the morning morphed through the afternoon and bled, inexorably toward a coming dusk, the burgeoning reality served to sharpen, rather than dull the senses.

It was becoming, uncomfortable. It was, like the very first tiny bubbles of steam air that broke the tension of the surface of the water as the boiling point approached.

As a group, they had now, only themselves. Their last communication, riddled and popping with static, had produced only a sporadic spit of words, of bits and pieces of phrases from which she, and a couple of the rest had attempted to fit together, like a jigsaw puzzle that demanded self-fulfillment.

A mention of elusive wildlife. The reference to remote caves and to unknown origins.

She recognized, and attempted to help others to realize, that aside from static being the constant, all they could discern from the staccato of that last transmission was that a new and frighteningly clever panic was afoot, that cautionary measures needed to be observed.

The solar winds had drowned out the following information. A word, or two – what she, and others she trusted thought – might be tokens, flitted amongst the thinning air space. A feeling that she alone understood – perhaps – that isolation was an important part of the verbal conveyance served to confuse even further – as it also baffled those closest about.

Wondering, muttering aloud, she asked, 'How much more isolated could we possibly be?'

The others, in response, literally shrugged. They were feeling, she was quite certain, a sort of ennui – a lassitude which generally results in times of deep uncertainty.

Any advancement along the thread of their path should probably be mitigated by the little they had figured out.

But how, and in what way might it be a beacon? It surely could not be, in its partiality, a compass of any kind.

Was it now their duty, their responsibility, as unwilling leaders, to find a way to be more pro-active in this journey? Towards a dark destination, only vaguely defined, that might provide the comfort of confidence – a confidence that they had long ago discarded.

It was not a question that either she – nor any of the rest of the group, was qualified to ask. For they had no rights of leadership. They had no destiny but to continue forward, to forge a path of a sort amongst the shadows of that unknown.

The hollow comfort of destiny.

A light, perhaps, at the end of this too long tunnel. . . . .

Faintly Sundown

The heat/warmth of a welcome exhaustion wash over me.

Sun and day is fading slowly into a misty sunset. Off to the left, far down in the deepest reach of the pasture the night dew starts to rise....drifting ghostly contrails float skywards.

My eyes are drawn to the setting sun, now a faintly defined orb, in the haze.

The chill is suddenly palpable as I rest, legs crossed at the ankles, worn cowboy boots caked in mud and dust.

Leaning back and into the supports that reach up to the porch overhang, I hear the tendrils of your lilting laughter.

'Autumn Leaves' whisper-sung by Eva Cassidy wafts out from the cool darkness of the cabin.

Duntz, the border collie mutt mix, lies beside me on the old warm boards of the porch. His paws occasionally stretch out to lightly touch my thigh, as he wants to remind that he's there and he's my ever friend.

My hand grips tightly to the tumbler carrying the blessed glass of hope....

And my thoughts reach out and around all the memories of you I hold dear to my heart. The ache, always there, always present, in my heart thrums against my rib cage.

And the singular question that haunts my every waking moment is

'Why?'

And on most every level of intellectuality I recognize the futility of the question.

That you're gone, now and forever, brings a constant mist to my eyes and pain to my heart....

Too young....so too very young - unfulfilled. And I ache and I hurt to hear your voice again.

Sun slips back and away into the covering mist and as twilight is flushed about me, I wonder why, am I, still......

A Knock At The Door

He shuffled awkwardly from the bedroom to the bathroom, his old slippers

the only sound in the pre-dawn dimness.

He paused at the threshold, as the shock of a twinge shot through his chest.

Grasping the smooth edge of the doorframe, his fingers finding a grip, he pulled himself more erect. In so doing, his chest rasped and he coughed, raggedly.

If it were not for the iron grip he had on the frame he might have been overtaken by the surge of heat and pain that shot down through his rib cage.

Eyes watering, vision blurring and feeling like he was slipping away he forced himself with a determined strength of will, to move through the doorway. With a slow pivot he turned so he could sit on the toilet. But it wasn't the toilet facilities he needed at that moment. It was simply a seat upon which to rest, to catch his breath.

Leaning sadly against the wall, his head drooping, cheek against the cool painted surface, he reached deep inside his lungs to find the edge of the thread of a clean, clear breath. As he sensed success, as he felt a small confidence start to surface, he was racked again by an explosive cough.

His eyes were tearing now, his vision cloudier. Raising his left hand to his forehead, the sweaty heat of his skin alarmed him.

Now, he was scared.

He hadn't been scared last night when he went to bed. He had congratulated himself with a small smile, on having coaxed himself through a day of sweats and coughing. But none of it had been alarming. He had managed to prepare his dinner over the protestations of Céline.

'I can do this, Sweetheart', he had said. 'It's a frozen pizza. What's the big deal – open box, stick in oven, sit, wait – eat. Done.'

'What's that? Yes, of course I'd like some chicken soup. But I don't have any and you're not driving all the way over here to bring me some. Besides, I'll bet you don't have some anyway, right?'

'Yeah – see? I knew it. Tomorrow. You'll come tomorrow. Even though you're not supposed to go out of the house, as you know. Besides which, my building is locked down. No visitors are allowed. Sorry.'

'Yes – yes, I'll be okay. It's a cold – just a bad cold. No – I'm not in pain.'

During this conversation he was with, one hand, opening the pizza box and clumsily removing the contents.'

He turned the oven to 425 and watched as the temperature bar started its climb.

'I'll be fine. Really. Yes – I'll keep my phone with me, beside me. And yes, I'll call you if I really need you. Promise. Okay – I love you and the kids. Good night.'

As he sat there, sweating, trancelike, the recall of those moments flashed by in a video re-run in his mind's eye.

And he was now, not feeling so cocky. No, not at all.

Another deep ripping cough tore at his lungs. He bent over, head between his legs pointing towards the tiled floor.

Suddenly he erupted with an upheaval of coughing and phlegm.

Wiping his eyes, his mouth, he looked down at the mess on the floor. Streaked with bright red blood the puddle shone brightly, glistening – kind of greasy looking.

His hands were shaking. He felt himself slipping, slipping away.

'Can't be ending like this' he thought. 'Just can't be.'

He forced himself upright and fumbling in his old dressing gown pocket pulled his phone out with his left hand.

It was taking most of his focus, most of his concentration to keep a firm grip on it.

Almost tumbled out of his grasp. Managing to hold on to it more tightly, with a blurred vision, he punched in number '1', Celine's speed dial.

His vision was fluttering. His heart felt like a blade was poking into it and all about it.

It took a moment – too long of a moment he was thinking, until she answered sleepily.

'Dad? Dad! Are you okay? What's wrong? Tell me! Are you alright? Say something – please – say something.'

Through the roaring in his ears he heard, or thought he heard, 'Greg! Greg! wake up – get your phone. Call 911. Get an ambulance over to Dad's right away.'

But he couldn't be sure. Maybe that's what he was hoping he was hearing.

The room started to fade, from the outside in. In a moment all he was seeing was a tiny circle of vision, a small circle of light, as life around him rapidly faded.

'Dad! DAD! Talk to me – just TALK to me – say something! Ambulance is coming – stay with me! Please God – stay with me.'

It took all his willpower to lift the phone towards his face.

'Yarrghh – erghh!' was what she heard.

She was weeping now – sobbing as she tried to elicit a response from him. Fear was knifing through her heart as she frantically tried to keep the phone in her hand and pull on some jeans and a sweater.

'Dad, Dad – we're coming. Just hang on. We'll be there soon!'

He coughed again – a rough coarse pain-filled tear from his chest.

It was all floating now. His vision was almost gone. The light in the room was now only a pin-point. A roaring, like rushing rapids filled his ears, flooded his brain.

Time drifted, pulling him along.

It was perhaps 5 minutes, maybe 25 minutes as he was carried along with the current of his life ebbing out of him.

The phone slipped, fell and hit the floor as he followed it down. Spread against the ceramic, his face among the blood and vomit, he opened his eyes, with one last determined effort, as he heard, a knock on the door.

AN ABRUPT CONVERSATION

'What are you doing in here?'

'Uh – I'm – I'm a guest. Why?'

'This is a restricted area – do you not, or can you not, read?'

'Uh – yeah – I can. I didn't see any signs though.'

'Oh! You're one of those are you?'

'One of – one of, what? Wait! Like I said, I'm a guest, and if I've done –'

'Stop!' she said. But she said it sooo imperiously. As in capital S capital T capital O capital P

STOP.

'You're one of those who either don't care, don't read, can't read – think that everything is

fair game – you just – you just, take what you want, go where you want. '

'No! No – honest. Not so – I was – guess I was kinda lost and I wondered over here.

I tried the door and it was unlocked – so I thought – just thought. . . . '

'You thought what? That you'd enter a restricted area? Looking for something to steal?

What? Are you, like an addict? You need to 'lift' things so you can sell them to buy illicit drugs?'

He wrung his hands, imploringly. He was completely at a loss.....his intentions had simply been to . . . .

'I only wanted to come in and see if the view down to the bay from here was even more spectacular than the view from the lounge....see, I was the first one here – when I came into the centre no one else had yet arrived and so...'

'STOP. Again, STOP. I need to call Security. Clearly you have suspicious intentions.'

She moved to click the mike on her shoulder.

'WAIT! WAIT – please – please – don't. '

She paused, her thumb on the microphone button. She raised an eyebrow, staring sternly at him.

'Wait for what?' she demanded.

'Here – here, let me me show you', as he reached inside his jacket pocket.

'Here – here's my invitation – today at 2:00 o'clock – VIP invitation – Hotel Beaulieu – and here – here's my ID – please!'

'Bring it over here – right here – now!' she commanded.

He sidled up to her, his left hand holding out the invitation card, along with what appeared to be a driver's license.

As she craned her head to look closely at it he snaked his right arm up and about her neck.

As she gasped and convulsed, he gave one sharp jerk and was rewarded with a sharp crack as he snapped her neck…..and then slowly, and gently, lowered her to the floor.

Yon Duck

The duck, one day, appeared. Perched on the concrete apron under the beach showers, she sat, disdainfully observing the passers-by. When anyone approached, she rose to her full height, wings outstretched, and fluttered a few yards away from the intruder. As most who spend any time in south Florida in the winter know, these Muscovy ducks are seen most everywhere. Black-feathered with crimson markings about their beak, they are an odd looking species.

In the days that followed, she became a curiosity and neighbours in our building took up regular surveillance. I christened her Yon Duck.

Meanwhile, progress encroached on Yon Duck's adopted habitat. Hollywood Beach was in the throes of a major renovation of the broad pedestrian walkway that borders the beach, known as the Broadwalk. Light standards and pavement were uprooted and removed to make way for a new wall and walking path and a ribbon of palms. Through it all, Yon Duck remained, and continued her dominion over any and all that approached.

From time to time, she would slowly waddle across the Broadwalk to take shelter under Donny's truck. Sometimes, when I left at 6:30 in the morning, I could see her there…snuggled up tight, wings tucked in. At other times we watched her cross the Broadwalk to pay a visit to Booby.

Booby is the most gorgeous Siamese cat – honey-colored with black flashes at her tail tip. Until Yon Duck arrived, Booby imperiously ruled this section of the Broadwalk.

Her master, Elmer, would often sit with her on the seawall that abounded the edge of their property and most who walked by would comment on her beauty.

Now, I haven't myself, seen this – but I'm told reliably as fact, that once in a while, Yon Duck makes this short journey down the sidewalk to the entrance to Boobys garden (a most delightful cultivation of palms, rich flora and potted plants which Elmer has constructed there), and, with a quick backwards glance, enter that enchanted space through the portico.

But, thus far, none of us has been privy to their conversation. Fortunately, and encouragingly, their discussions have been conducted in quietude and peacefully. There has been, thus far, no furious flapping of wings, nor enraged yowls from Booby.

Determined to respect their privacy, we, who stand around and watch, will usually drift away. For we don't ever know how long these meetings might last. Thus, none of us have ever actually seen Yon Duck emerge from the Enchanted Garden.

But – she does….and all of a sudden, there she is again. Poised beneath the showerhead.

Some of us have discovered that she likes to drink from freshly pooled water which collects on the shower apron. So, we will tentatively approach her, in order to activate the faucet.

She, of course, moves away. None of us get particularly close. Except, perhaps, Carroll. But then, she is possessed of a mystical magical ability to commune with all nature of feathered creatures.

In any event, Yon Duck, will, for hours sometimes, remain there. Oftentimes with one leg tucked up under her, she sits, sphinx-like, watching the passers-by.

In the last week, things have become somewhat more serious. Seems a good local soul felt there was imminent danger in her resting place. Threats from the trenchers and earth-movers which were employed in the beautification of our Broadwalk. So, the Fish, Game and Wildlife folks were called to rescue her.

Our friend TV called us to let us know. We anxiously walked out onto the catwalk corridor of our building . From the fifth floor, we watched, giggling, as three of these well-intentioned souls attempted to take Yon Duck into protective custody.

As soon as they got within 3 or 4 paces of her, she raised her magnificent wings, and skip-flew ten or fifteen yards away from them. This went on for a good half hour. At the end of that session, the score was Yon Duck 1 – Visitors ZERO.

They must have given up and left. Yon Duck remained.

And, she, thankfully, still remains. Although, just the other morning in the early dawn light, while sitting at my computer, I glanced out to the south-west, and, flying low, just over the tree-tops, was Yon Duck. She beat a path just beyond my window, headed quite obviously back to her post of choice – apparently for her morning shower.

On a Monday night, three days following Thanksgiving, it was a particularly windy and blustery. Although the skies were clear, the winds were wild – blasting in from the east off the Atlantic.

I went outside to check.

She was there – I wasn't quite sure at first....I saw only a dark bump on the concrete apron of the shower post. So, I got our binoculars and double-checked. Yes – that was definitely her.

Yon Duck, drawn in tight, motionless against the relentless assault of the wind.

 She was waiting – heaven knows for what, but – she seemed to be waiting.

It was worrisome to see – I knew we would all like to have given her shelter.

And, yet – I realized she must be there, because that's where she wanted to be.

But she had no protection. The winds chuffed in off the whitecaps, a direct frontal blitz, which whipped the sand up and around her.

But there she remained. Like a sailor of old – braced up against the mast, fearlessly facing a ragged sea. Defiant, it would seem. And, yet – what could I do? If I had approached her, she would have flitted away. And, even if I could have gotten close enough to throw a blanket about her, what then?

No….that couldn't ever work. It was best to leave her alone. She always returned there, day after day.

Arriving home the other night she was in the middle of the road outside the garage entry. And, Elmer was out there also. Glass of beer in hand.

'Hey Elmer! You having a beer with Yon Duck?'

He replied, 'We're not THAT friendly yet….but I'm workin on her.'

'Good luck', I replied. 'Just don't get her drunk – unfair advantage and all that, what?'

A few days later TV dropped by and in bringing us up to date on the goings-on in and around our building, he recounted how, a day or so ago, he had seen Elmer standing out on the Broadwalk.

He strolled up to him, said, 'Hey - howzit goin' Elmer?'

Elmer, it seems was, as he is from time to time, standoffish. He sorta grunted.

TV, never one to be discouraged by rejection, said again, 'Hey Elmer - whussup? How's the duck? You seen her?'

Elmer, in a rather cranky tone, replied, 'Duck had a run in with a dog - with a big dog.'

TV asked, 'Is she okay? What happened?'

Elmer replied, 'Duck's gone....she's gone, man.'

TV: 'But, where'd she go? Do you think she's alright?'

Elmer: 'Dint you hear me, man? Duck had a run-in with a big dog - duck lost....duck's gone, man. She's just gone!'

TV recognised he would get no further information. When Elmer is disposed that way, he's not nice to be around.

I listened to this distressing update. I had been hoping, really, that Yon Duck had maybe just taken a break from the rigors of construction turmoil, all the dust and noise and such. I hoped, as did we all, that given a few days, Yon Duck would again return to this, her new roost.

The news, saddened me deeply. I imagined all sorts of scenarios - big aggressive dog bearing down on a quiet, gentle unsuspecting Yon Duck......a furious attempt at flight - a frenzied beating of wings, and the BigDog all the while wheeling about in the soft sand, pouncing, snapping - grabbing, finally, Yon Duck. I couldn't bear to think more about it.......

During the 30 mile drive to work the next morning I felt very unsettled and rather disheartened by this unexpected development. Most of the building's residents had come to adopt her, spiritually if not physically. It was depressing to think that nasty danger had befallen her.

When I arrived at the office I turned into the empty parking lot and slowly cruised to the far end of the lot, close to the building entry. At 6:30 in the morning mine was usually the only car in the lot.

Getting out of the car my attention was distracted by a dark shape just ahead and to my left. Just at the end of a row of bushes. In attempting to make out what appeared as a familiar sort of shape, I took a step in that direction. With a sudden flurry of beating wings the shape took flight – for a few yards. As it settled, turning back towards me, it tucked one leg up under her belly, and gazed at me, sphinx-like.

Damn if it wasn't my best hope come true – it was surely, Yon Duck.

Good for her.

And good, for all of us.

Sadly she hasn't again returned to the beach – leastwise not our beach. On the other hand, I now regularly see her in the early morning light when I get to work. The confirmation of life and determination gives me strength and inspiration each time.

Desmond Dak

This is the autobiography of one Desmond Dak.

Which is really Desmond Dakschmuller – with the doubleDot over the ú'.

I am the illegitimate child of Howard Hughes and Hugh Hefner….

Now that may sound weird - but believe me it is, in actual fact, far more weird than you could possible imagine.

My friends – of which I claim two – call me Zak….. we'll get to that. And we'll get to my friends in due time.

I am, independently wealthy and am referred to in certain quarters (Benin for one)

as that JewboyFromThe Bronx.

I do not work at anything as I don't have to.

But I do, work.

In any event, my last assignment required the elimination of a PowderPuff girl

who had betrayed her best boss…… and I must confess, this was one of my most difficult assignments.

You have, no doubt, heard of snuff films…… usually erotic, or pornographic efforts, where at the exact point of the onset of a woman's orgasm, her lover/partner, kills her.

The French call it the 'little death'…..the orgasm that is.

This might be best referred to as the BigDeath…..'cause that was my assignment.

Very precisely..... to kill her at that exact moment. And, so – I did.

The aftermath was, shall we say, most unusual. For a man, of course. The shudders that signal the oncoming climax, become weaker as a frantic understanding takes hold in her eyes...... as her vagina relaxes into acceptance – well – you can imagine for yourselves how it might be.

Ain't pretty, as it is said.

Two hours later I was waiting to board my flight to Jakarta when my phone chirped.

I kinda knew who it would be.

....and I was not surprised and in no way, disappointed.

'Went well?' the deep sonorous voice asked.

'Doesn't it always?', I replied testily.

Not too testily, for, that might have set him off......something you never want to do.

Leastwise if it is you who is to become the target of his anger.

'You know me....', I asked with an unvoiced but clearly understood, chuckle.

'Prince among men....Prince of Death...'

'Shut the fuck up. You were paid – very well also – to do a job. You have no right

nor license to act arrogantly. Especially to me – especially, NOT to me......understood?'

'Yessir……clear.'

'So – where you headed?'

He never asked THAT before.

'Thai Bay Xanadu', I responded quickly…..

'Ah yes……know it, I do….well enjoy your respite. I will reach out if and when there is a need. The agreed upon transaction has been completed.'

Radio silence. He had disconnected.

Not sure why I was feeling somewhat unbalanced, unsettled…..

But I was.

'Fuck it', I told myself. 'You're now richer than your wildest dreams ever imagined.

Go have one of those Wellington singles…..whilst thee awaits thy flight'.

I liked to do that sometimes…..that Skakespearian bullshit. Fun. Defiant, kinda….

Twenty minutes later my flight was called. The gentle scald of the single malt rested neatly against my gums.

'Need to find more of where that came from', I said to myself as I grabbed my backpack and headed towards the gate.

Some six hours later I was gently nudged and heard, 'Sorry sir – need to fasten the seat belt, get the chair upright….we're on final approach.'

I started……jerked a bit. Was embarrassed that had…..looked up into the most startling blue eyes set in a rich mahogany angel face.

Mouth and head feeling uncomfortably fuzzy, I blinked – once or twenty times.

'Can I get a glass of water? Or anything? Please?'

I hated when I was whiny….

'I'll try and get something back to you – no promises.', she smiled.

'Man….now there's a promise I'd like to collect on', I thought.

'Of course – fine – thank you'

I struggled upright – pushed the button to pop the seat back straight. Rubbed my eyes, rubbed my head – vigorously. Looked out the window….saw only grey wisps of cloud or fog…..couldn't tell which.

Looked at my watch – loved that watch. The latest Apple watch…it was, so elegant.

More elegant than possible, because like all Apple efforts….they never tried to be elegant – they just – were.

I had selected the solar system watch face…..it showed a little green dot to indicate where in the world I presently was…and I it showed the line of demarcation between sunrise and darkness…..or sunset and darkness as it might apply.

I saw that where we were globally positioned was maybe an hour before dark.

As the nightline approached the lightline……fascinating – always.

'So', I thought to myself, 'Landing in about twenty minutes….. half an hour to clear customs, get bag, get a cab. Should get to the hotel about 40 minutes after that

And that's pretty much how it happened.

Have to say, The Thai Bay Emerald Hotel is one of the world's finest.

From the moment I stepped out of the shuttle limousine, under the broad canopy wrapped in graceful palms, to the almost inaudible hiss as the large glass doors greeted me in opening – to the intricate marble inserts in the rich parquet flooring – everything about it whispered, 'best taste'. Didn't scream it – didn't have to – was the way that it was- quiet elegance with all guests, staff and personnel complicit in its messaging.

At the desk was a choice check-in agents – all women, each more exotic than the next. I didn't even attempt a choice – moved directly to the very closest one. And of course was treated to a dazzling and thoroughly sincere smile.

'Mr. Desmond – so nice for you to visit us again. You know we will do our very best to care for you during your stay. Do you expect it to be again for a two week period?'

Any attempt at flirtatious behaviour would result in a visit from Guest Services who would discreetly inform me that all staff, was off-limits, to all guests.

And so in my best business voice I replied, 'How kind of you to enquire. However as I have recently completed a most arduous assignment I expect I will want to rest up here for at least three weeks – maybe four.'

A gracious smile and a nod of her head resulted in a key card being instantly held out to me.

'Khxbkhuṇ' I offered in reply, turning to move towards the elevators.

Reaching my room on the 27th floor, the bellman entered with my bag, fussed about the room a little and turned to leave at which point I held out a generous tip.

It was important for him to be impressed so that he would pass on to his co-workers that I am a valued client.

After spending twenty minutes or so sorting and unpacking, I made myself a G&T, sat in the comfortable lounge chair which faced the doors, with a view across the terrasse and out through the glass balustrade to the ocean and its horizon in the misty, heated distance.

Putting my feet up, I sipped at the icy cool mixture and in a short time fell deeply asleep.

Not sure how long I was sleeping but when the room phone rang and awakened me, the horizon was no longer visible as inky night had fallen.

Somewhat groggily I rose, made my way to the desk, picked up the phone and heard,

'We know where you are. No point in running – we know you did not complete the mission – likely out of some misguided sense of chivalry – and now, for that, you will pay.'

an emiLlyburKke

The next to last time he saw her she glided, like a whisper on a cloud, to stand next to him at the raised checkout counter.

Looking to his right he was overwhelmed by her soft beauty

Hair the colour of honey, with air in it, fell down and around her exquisite face to frame it like a wanted poster. Soft, lustrous, curving hair that reached her shoulders where it ended in a necklace of tight ringlets.

She looked straight ahead to a space he couldn't see. Mouthing soft words to whom he could not hear. Her eyes a liquid brown like amber fired but tinged with flecks of gold, were clear and set off the caramel colour of her skin. An impossible mouth, lips moistly inviting, moved as in a mantra.

In her hands she held a device that both pulsed and twinkled with diamond lights. Her elbows on the counter, she stood looking straight ahead.

He could see that she wore only a pair of tight-fitting cut-off blue jean shorts the frayed fringes of which rippled in the soft breeze.

As his attention intensified, she became suddenly aware of his presence, and turning to face him, she smiled generously and warmly.

She extended her right hand to him and said, in a murmur, 'It is still lovely to meet of you. I am, an Emily Burke.Can I offer and deliver to you any assisting today?'

'I too am of pleased to make of you an acquaintance' he replied.

'In the procedure of out-checking I will be seeking guidance for my trip. Might that be of interest to you?'

He was blasted with a dazzling smile that revealed perfect dental work. And a tongue tipped with claret that danced as she spoke. 'A trip is where I've come from and will excited be to embark on another one still. Where do you want of your travel to be taking you?'

'It is an outbound galaxy thrust that requires my inspection.

A crew which is part of my reward is to be meeting me upon arrival. It is far to the downward spiral into X-1Dalmatian that I need to negotiate.'

'Sounds it to be of interest and some excitement. I have skillsets that have been generously provided me of which you might find useful. An excellent pilot of most craft is also a part of my CV. You have a departure point and time assigned?'

'I do', he replied.'It is at dawnstart tomorrow date. Which', he paused,'Allows for a night-time of preparation. Of which you might be interested?'

'With clearance required for my outbound I could find you in about five times. Is that agreeable for your times?'

'Tis.....mais, supper times have been established in my protocols......meeting you back in 2.66 times would be agreeable?'

He closed his left eye, blinked once, and replied, 'I can see of the time required that such would be amenable to my purpose. We meet, should we again, in 3.0?'

'Parfait!', she exclaimed gaily. With a small clap of her hands she rotated on her left foot in a perfect circle, and launched herself off towards the portal.

'I should have expected nothing less....'he thought to himself.

Acceptance

Throughout the whole of the night as we continued northward she sat wedged into the corner of her seat, rather rigidly upright, with her left leg angled across the bench seat. She, at the same time, appeared to be both poised and yet complacent. Prepared and yet completely comfortable. Content and yet indifferent.

I on the other hand, as the miles unwound behind us, felt my energy morph from the extreme high of all the frenzied actions and surrounding events to a settling in. To a settling in to a curiosity as to where we might now be heading.

That feeling had only begun to emerge once we had cleared the border, once we crossed into Canada. Perhaps it was based on a sense that we were maybe now unreachable.

Or if not unreachable, unlikely to be pursued further.

The hour or so spent in the old trucker's diner about a hundred miles back seems to have restored a degree of connectivity between her battered soul and the beauty of the world around her. The majestic sweep of the towering pines, the crystal choppiness of the lakes we passed by.....the cold, clear crispness of the northern Canadian air.....it was ever so regenerative I'm sure of it.

When we did stop at times, pulling over to a lookout, we would exit the car and find a place to rest - against a tree, on a bench....leaning against a rail. She even, once, leaned into me.

And soft wind and gentle air would wash around us. The velvet silence a coccoon.

Watching her as she sat so deathly still, with that slight upturn at the corner of her mouth, with her unwavering stare set to the middle distance, I was not - and realized I could never be - certain that she knew she was with me, finally.

And to, for more than a few seconds, think that - wish that - she actually cared......that is beyond any reasonable hope or expectation I might have.

But I was content. No, more than content. I was smooth - all smooth, inside and out.

Her otherworldly beauty embraced her physical being like a time-worn cape. To be here, to be wherever tomorrow takes us, is beyond my sense of balance.

I knew, finally, that 'whatever it takes'- would be my life compass from this time on.

And so the question that will greet me every time I awake - from a nap, from a semi-comatose binge - or from a full night of sleep, is likely to be....'whatever might I expect from this....... and if it all gets taken away from me suddenly, how will I manage to survive?'

And my answer now and forever will be

'I don't care......really'

Perfect. are we?

Chirpy, bright like crystals, came the question.

'And how are you today?'

> 'Me?', I asked, wondering.
> 'Why, I'm almost perfect!'

Honest eruption of a smile, wrapped in a giggle.

'Perfect? Perfect are we?'

> 'Well, no – not yet.
> I said, "Almost, perfect"

She, looked down then. Her gaze re-focused to the crossword puzzle spread across the old wooden counter, next to the very old brass keyed cash register.

Sheepishly, somewhat, I coughed – to regain her attention.

I know – nervy.

> 'But today is still young. Come late afternoon -
> I may just actually be rather closer – to perfect.'

'Good luck with that!'

'Well, one can only hope.'

Lifting my chin from where I had been gazing, sheepishly at my shoes
I looked at her again then turned to exit the café.

As I did I felt, rather than heard, sent from her anthracite eyes,

'Aren't we quite the fool today?'

About the Author

From a first career spent in the built environment and its constituent disciplines -architecture, interior design, industrial design, graphic design - he transitioned into the world of writing.

With his first novel completed, and its sequel well over half finished, he is writing/developing five other novels simultaneously.

Teaching and leading courses in Creative Writing still leaves him time and energy to engage himself in a number of different writing groups spread from Paris to New York. Toronto to Montreal and other cities.

This publication is the first of a proposed series that focuses on poetry, flash fiction and short stories.

Michael Moore M.A.
https://michaelXmoore.com
or
https://WritingMatters.Online

Made in the USA
Columbia, SC
03 June 2024